UMOPL Series Volumes:

ISBN 1-879763-11-7

LUSHOOTSEED READER

WITH

INTRODUCTORY GRAMMAR

This snapshot of Edward Sam with Ethel Kitsap Sam is the only photograph of Mr. Sam known to exist.
Provided by William Edward (sʔadacut) Sam, his nephew and foster son.

LUSHOOTSEED READER

WITH

INTRODUCTORY GRAMMAR

Volume I

Four Stories from Edward Sam

THOM HESS

UNIVERSITY OF MONTANA OCCASIONAL PAPERS IN LINGUISTICS No. 11, 1995

First Published March 1995

UMOPL — A series dedicated to the study
of the Native languages of the Northwest.

SERIES EDITORS
    Anthony Mattina, University of Montana (li_am@selway.umt.edu)
    Timothy Montler, University of North Texas (montler@jove.acs.unt.edu)

Address all correspondence to:
    UMOPL — Linguistics Laboratory
    The University of Montana
    Missoula, MT 59812

Hess, Thom
    Lushootseed Reader With Introductory Grammar
    UMOPL No. 11

ISBN 1-879763-11-7

Library of Congress Catalog Number: 95-060060

Typeset with WordPerfect 5.1
    at the Linguistics Laboratory
    University of Montana

Printed at Summer Institute of Linguistics
    Dallas

CONTENTS

FOREWORD

It is with pleasure, and pride in my people that I present this first volume of the *Lushootseed Reader*. It includes four of the ancient stories of our forebearers along with a grammar of their language. The stories were recited by Edward Sam and tape-recorded here at Tulalip exactly thirty years ago.

Throughout the 1960's a number of other stories and reminiscences were told by Elizabeth Krise and Martha Lamont. These too were tape-recorded along with more texts by Mr. Sam. Two further volumes of this reader are in preparation which will make these other stories available to our young people at Tulalip and to the world at large.

In November of 1961 Thom Hess, then a graduate student in linguistics at the University of Washington, began the systematic study of our language. It was he who made the recordings with the knowledge and approval of the Tribal leadership at that time. In those days there still lived at Tulalip several score people who spoke Lushootseed better than they did English and a few who hardly knew English at all. These were people whose formative years were spent in the old ways and whose parents had grown up before the whites began to settle in this region. By 1961 the material culture of the Lushootseed had vanished; but for the elders the non-material facets of Lushootseed culture remained a vital part of their daily lives. They had quested for spirit-power in primeval forests now gone. They knew intimately the animals, plants and other beings of the land. In their minds they still heard the old songs and they could still recite the ancient stories passed down from long, long ago before Changer transformed the world in preparation for human habitation.

This reader attempts to provide a glimpse of one facet of that former life by enabling those interested to read a few of the old stories in the medium in which they were created.

Henry kʷil'əmqidəm Gobin
Cultural Resources Manager
The Tulalip Tribes
26 October 1993

INTRODUCTION

Wedged between the mountains of the Olympic Peninsula to the west and the Cascade Mountain Range to the east there extends southward a 160 mile long finger of the Pacific Ocean called Puget Sound. This body of water is filigreed by many, many islands, inlets and channels. Similarly the (formerly) heavily forested land is cut into intricate patterns by many rivers and streams flowing from the mountains into the sound. Lakes large and small speckle the land in counter point to the many islands that dot the sound. The shore line alternates between steep bluffs and low lying beaches. Travelling upstream either east or west, the rivers quickly narrow to fast flowing mountain streams with spectacular waterfalls. Wherever one looks on a clear day, there is water bounded by forest green with snow covered mountains in the background. This for eons has been home to the Lushootseed.

Lushootseed is the English name for the language and the people who speak it. It derives from the native name dxʷləšucid. The prefix dxʷ- together with the suffix -ucid means *language*. The root (or core) of the word is ləš which some scholars believe to be related to the ancient native word for *people*, (rendered in English as Salish). Today *Salish* is the name given to the twenty-three distinct but related languages to which Lushootseed belongs.

Before reservation relocation there were many slight differences in accent and vocabulary which threaded among the numerous original villages. Most of these differences are now lost but enough survive to easily divide the language into a northern and a southern variety. The northern division has a major subgroup which separates the speech at Swinomish and along the Skagit River downstream of the Sauk from the rest of Northern Lushootseed. These differences as well as smaller, more limited ones are pointed out in the introductory grammar as they arise.

This reader begins with twenty-two lessons divided into three units which lay the grammatical foundation for reading these texts. As often as possible the lessons are arranged so that the student discovers the various grammatical facts for himself/herself. Those points not covered in these three units are dealt with in the glossary or in footnotes to the texts.

The four texts included in this first volume are ancient stories (called syəyəhub in the north and sx̌ʷiʔab in the south). They were told by Mr. Edward Sam of the Tulalip

Reservation in the summer of 1963. In the telling Mr. Sam used a fairly simple and straight forward style in deference to the researcher's fledgling ability in Lushootseed at that time. In spite of this simplicity, the same characterization and humour is encountered in these stories as in other versions which have more complex sentences. They are ideal for the beginning student.

The accompanying cassette of Mr. Sam's story telling is made from the original reel to reel tapes recorded in 1963. However, these originals were not made under ideal acoustic conditions, and the subsequent thirty years have not been kind to them either. One story in particular has suffered a considerable distortion in vocal pitch. Nevertheless, in all cases the diction is easily intelligible. This cassette provides the student with an opportunity to hear what Lushootseed sounded like in former times.

The first and second volumes each have four stories. Four is the culturally significant number among the Tulalip people and others of Northern Lushootseed ancestry just as three and seven are the culturally weighted numbers in European tradition. By presenting these texts in sets of four, in a small way one custom of the ancient Northern Lushootseed is maintained. (Among the Southern Lushootseed the equivalent number is five.)

It should be noted that the grammar included with this reader is intended to help one learn to read Lushootseed in the original as quickly as possible. It is not designed to help someone learn to speak the language. For that purpose other materials are available. Nevertheless, for those who may know elementary linguistic terminology, a few remarks on the sounds of Lushootseed are given in the Appendix.

Various articles and books about this or that facet of the Lushootseed people exist but none provides a particularly detailed description. The best source of information on the former life of the Lushootseed speaking peoples is to be found in volume 7 of the *Handbook of North American Indians* published by the Smithsonian Institution, Washington, D.C. 1990. The article therein by Wayne Suttles and Barbara Lane entitled the *Southern Coast Salish* is excellent. Those interested should begin their background reading on the Lushootseed with this article and its bibliography.

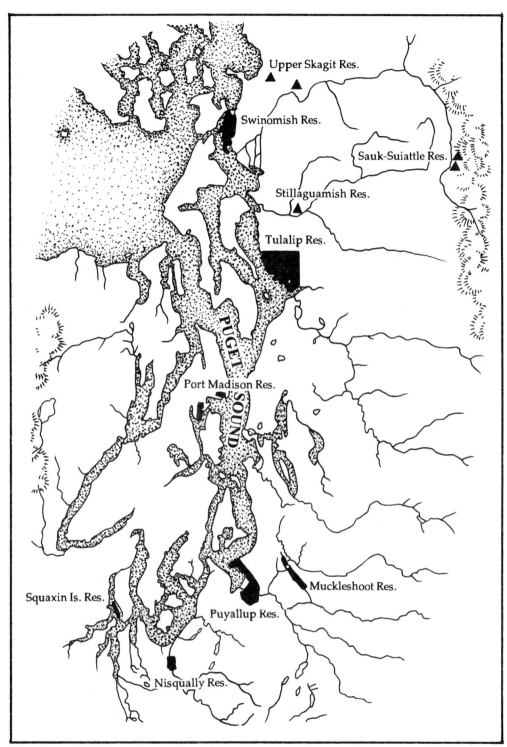

Lushootseed and surrounding territory

UNIT ONE

IDENTIFYING SEMANTIC ROLES

IN

THE MAIN CLAUSE

LESSON ONE

-txʷ, agent, patient

Compare the following six sentences with each other and with their English translations. Then answer the questions below. (English words in square brackets do not correspond to any word in the Lushootseed sentence. They are simply required by English grammar.)

1. ʔuʔux̌ʷ ti čačas*.[1]   The boy went.
2. ʔuʔux̌ʷtxʷ ti čačas.   [Someone] took the boy somewhere.
3. ʔuʔəƛ'txʷ ti čačas.   [Someone] brought the boy.
4. ʔut'ukʷ ti čačas.   The boy went home.
5. ʔut'ukʷtxʷ ti čačas.   [Someone] took the boy home.
6. ʔuʔəƛ' ti čačas.   The boy came.

Where does the **verb** (the action word) come in a Lushootseed sentence -- first or last? _first_. What does ti čačas mean? _the boy_. In sentences numbered 1, 4, and 6 does ti čačas perform the action; that is, in 1, 4, and 6 is ti čačas the **agent** (the doer)? _yes_. Is ti čačas the agent in sentences 2, 3, and 5 or is it the **patient** (the one to whom some act is done)? _patient_. On the following blank write what it is in these Lushootseed sentences that tells the reader or listener whether ti čačas is agent or patient. _txʷ_. What does ʔut'ukʷ mean? _go home_.

1.1. In sentences of the type written above, Lushootseed does not have words matching the English *he, she, it,* or *they* (nor *him, her,* or *them* either). Where the English translation requires one of these words, *someone* or *something* is used (unless the context makes clear that *he* or *she*, etc. is appropriate). Therefore, sentence 2 above, for example, could equally well be translated as <u>He</u> *took the boy.* <u>She</u> *took the boy.* <u>They</u> *took the boy.*

---

[1]An asterisk (*) following a word calls the student's attention to the fact that that particular word is limited to certain parts of the Lushootseed speaking territory. In other regions other words or other pronunciations are used. These differences are described in sections called *dialect differences*.

3

1.2. To write or print the letter λ̓ (called **lambda**), first make the long diagonal line, \ ; then add to it a short diagonal line going the other way, λ. Next cross the longer line with one parallel to and about the same length as the shorter line, λ̵ . Finally, write a small hook just above the three lines already in place, λ̓ .

1.3. To write or print the letter ə (called schwa -- sometimes spelled shwa), begin at the top and end inside: ꓛ, ɔ , ə .

1.4. Dialect differences. The word čačas is a Northern Lushootseed form. Throughout the Southern Lushootseed region the final sound is different. There, the word is čačaš.

    Study the next six sentences, those numbered 7 through 12, and contrast them with the first six presented above.

7. ʔuʔux̌ʷ.	[Someone] went.
8. ʔuʔux̌ʷtxʷ.	[Someone] took [someone] somewhere.
9. ʔuʔəƛ̓txʷ.	[Someone] brought [someone].
10. ʔut̓ukʷ.	[Someone] went home.
11. ʔut̓ukʷtxʷ.	[Someone] took [someone] home.
12. ʔuʔəƛ̓.	[Someone] came.

1.5. As this second set of sentences shows, in Lushootseed it is possible to omit entirely specific mention of an agent or patient leaving only the verb. Such verb-only sentences are common and considered to be good grammar and good Lushootseed style. Context makes clear who is acting on whom.

    The point made in section **1.1.** applies here as well. Sentence 11, for example, could be translated as _He_ took _her_ home. _She_ took _him_ home. _They_ took _her_ home. . . .

1.6. Exercise. Translate the following into Lushootseed:

1. [He] went.   *ʔuʔux̌ʷ*
2. [She] took the boy home.   *ʔut̓ ukʷu txʷ*
3. [Someone] brought the boy.   *ʔuʔ əƛ̓ txʷ ti čačas*
4. [Someone] brought [him].   *ʔu əƛ̓ txʷ*
5. [He] took [her] somewhere.   *ʔu ukʷ txʷ*
6. [She] came.   *ʔu əƛ̓*

7. [He] went home. ʔutʔ ukʷ .

8. [He] took [them] home. ʔutʔ ukʷ Tχʷ .

9. The boy came. ʔuʔ əƛʔ .

10. The boy went. ʔuʔ uχʷ .

11. [Someone] took the boy home. ʔutʔ ukʷ tkʷ .

12. The boy went home. ʔuʔ ukʷ .

LESSON TWO
čəd, čəxʷ, čəɬ, čələp

Examine the following six sentences comparing them with their translations and contrasting them with each other and the sentences in lesson one.

1. ʔuʔuxʷ čəd.   I went.

2. ʔuʔuxʷtxʷ čəd ti čʼačʼas.   I took the boy somewhere.

3. ʔuʔəƛ'txʷ čəd ti čʼačʼas.   I brought the boy.

4. ʔutʼukʷ čəɬ.   We went home.

5. ʔutʼukʷtxʷ čəɬ ti čʼačʼas.   We took the boy home.

6. ʔuʔəƛ' čəɬ.   We came.

What does čəd mean? _____ _I_ _____. What does čəɬ mean? _____ _we_ _____. Do these two words express the agent or the patient in their sentences? _____ _agent_ _____. Write the Lushootseed for the following:

I went home. _____ ʔutʼukʷ čəd _____.

We brought the boy. _____ ʔuʔəƛ'txʷ čəɬ ti čʼačʼas _____.

I took the boy home. _____ ʔutʼukʷtxʷ čəd ti čʼačʼas _____.

2.1. In printing or writing Lushootseed, be certain to make clearly distinct from each other the letters t and ɬ. Make the t with a single vertical stroke and a straight cross line, †; while ɬ should be a long, thin loop with a wavy cross line, Ⱡ.

Study the following sentences:

7. ʔuʔəƛ' čəxʷ.   You came.

8. ʔuʔuxʷ čəxʷ ʔu   Did you go?

9. ʔutʼukʷtxʷ čəxʷ ʔu ti čʼačʼas. Did you take the boy home?

10. ʔuʔuxʷtxʷ čələp ʔu ti čʼačʼas. Did you folks take the boy somewhere?

11. ʔuʔəƛ' čələp.   You folks came.

6

x̌ʷ čələp ʔu.   Did you folks go?

ƛ’ ʔu ti č’ač’as.   Did the boy come?

.’txʷ ʔu ti č’ač’as.   Did [someone] bring the boy?

little word ʔu mean? _____. (Such little words are called
nguists.) Where in the sentence does it occur? _____
    What is the difference in meaning between čəxʷ and čələp? _____
_____.

; James and the Douay English translations of the Bible there are,
words *thou* and *ye*. If you do not already know their meanings, find out
sh dictionary or other source which one, *thou* or *ye*, corresponds to
' and which to Lushootseed čələp. Cross out the inappropriate English

u   ye

ı   ye.

nark is not a part of Standard Lushootseed spelling; nor is it necessary.
article ʔu makes very clear whether or not a sentence is interrogative.

tive particle is almost always pronounced as though it were spelled
    ʔu. Consequently, it tends to merge with the preceding word. One
pu. Only in careful speech does the ear detect a clear 'break' between
ınd ʔu. The spelling, however, is always the same.

ıe world's alphabets, such as the Greek, Roman, and Cyrillic, have
's called capitals. The Lushootseed alphabet is like the Hebrew,
Gurmukhi, Hangul, and many, many others in not having capital

.....ate the following into Lushootseed:

1. [Someone] went. _____.

2. I brought the boy.   _____.

3. We came. _____.

4. Did you folks take the boy home? _____.

5. Did you folks take [him] home? _____.

6. Did [she] take the boy home? _____.

7. Did you take [them] somewhere? _____.

8. Did you take [someone] home? _____.

LESSON THREE

-d and -b, ti and tsi

Compare the sentences immediately below with each other, with their translations, and with the sentences in Lesson One.

1. ʔugʷəč'əd tsi č'ač'as.   [Someone] looked for the girl.

2. ʔugʷəč'əb tsi č'ač'as.   The girl looked for [something / someone].

3. ʔuqʷʼəlb tsi č'ač'as.   The girl roasted [something].

4. ʔuqʷʼəld ti sʔuladxʷ*.   [Someone] roasted a² salmon.

5. ʔuhədʔiw'd ti sqʷəbayʔ.   [Someone] took/brought the dog into the house.

6. ʔuhədʔiw'b ti sqʷəbayʔ.   The dog went/came into the house.

3.1. What is the difference in meaning between ti č'ač'as (in Lessons One and Two) and tsi č'ač'as(of this lesson)? _____.
Note that this difference is signalled in the little word corresponding to *the* (or *a*) in English and not in the **noun** č'ač'as itself. (A noun can be conveniently thought of as the word for a person, animal, object, place, or abstract notion.) Three Lushootseed nouns have been presented thus far. Write the English meanings beside each one.

sʔuladxʷ _____

č'ač'as   _____

sqʷəbayʔ _____

3.2. Hundreds of Lushootseed nouns begin with the letter (and sound) s. This s is a prefix which in many cases has become inseparable and could be treated as part of the noun **stem** itself. However, the glossary at the end of this reader does not list these nouns under the initial s because there are so many of them. Therefore, nouns beginning with s followed by a second consonant are to be found listed under that second consonant. Thus, sʔuladxʷ is to be found under ʔ and sqʷəbayʔ under qʷ.

_____

²The distinction in English between *the* and *a* does not exist in Lushootseed. In Lesson Fifteen the significance of ti (and tsi) is presented in detail.

Three new sets of verbs occur in this lesson. Note their **suffixes** (endings). Does an agent or patient follow the suffix -d? _____. In this respect is -txʷ like -d or -b? _____. In Lesson One there are three verbs that have no suffixes at all. Does the following noun (when expressed) represent the agent or the patient? _____. In this respect are the suffixless verbs in Lessons One and Two like those ending in -d or those ending in -b? _____.

Study the following six sentences (numbered 7 through 12) comparing them to those numbered 1 through 6 above in this lesson and to the sentences in Lesson Two.

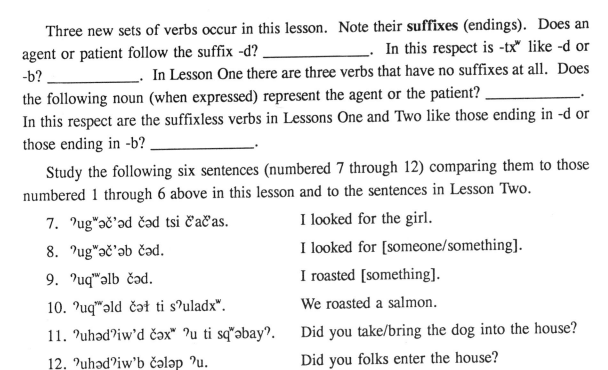

7.	ʔugʷəč'əd čad tsi č'ač'as.	I looked for the girl.
8.	ʔugʷəč'əb čad.	I looked for [someone/something].
9.	ʔuqʷʷəlb čad.	I roasted [something].
10.	ʔuqʷʷəld čəł ti sʔuladxʷ.	We roasted a salmon.
11.	ʔuhədʔiw'd čəxʷ ʔu ti sqʷəbayʔ.	Did you take/bring the dog into the house?
12.	ʔuhədʔiw'b čələp ʔu.	Did you folks enter the house?

3.3. As in Lesson Two, so too here the words čad, čəł, čəxʷ, and čələp express agent. Stated another way, these four words designate the doer whether or not there is a verb suffix and whether that suffix be -txʷ, -d, or -b. A noun, on the other hand, (that is one of the words preceded by ti or tsi) always stands for the patient when the verb takes the suffix -txʷ or -d; but it represents the agent when the verb has the suffix -b or no suffix at all. In the beginning the student may find it easier to keep straight the difference between how čad-words and nouns function in a sentence by imagining the existence of a čad-word for *he, she, it, they, someone,* etc. This imaginary word is indicated by [ ] in sentence (e) below.

(a)	ʔugʷəč'əd čad ti sqʷəbayʔ.	I looked for the dog.
(b)	ʔugʷəč'əd čəł ti sqʷəbayʔ.	We looked for the dog.
(c)	ʔugʷəč'əd čəxʷ ti sqʷəbayʔ.	You looked for the dog.
(d)	ʔugʷəč'əd čələp ti sqʷəbayʔ.	You folks looked for the dog.
(e)	ʔugʷəč'əd [ ] ti sqʷəbayʔ.	[Someone] looked for the dog.

3.4. When one of the four čad-words appears in a sentence and there is no noun, then as far as English translations are concerned, -- and **only then** -- it makes no difference whether a verb ends in -d or -b. Compare the following two sentences:

(f) ʔugʷəč'əd čəd.   I looked for [something].

(g) ʔugʷəč'əb čəd.   I looked for [something].

3.5. Dialect differences. The Northern Lushootseed word sʔuladxʷ corresponds to sčədadxʷ in Southern Lushootseed. (See the introduction to this reader for a discussion of Lushootseed dialect distributions.)

Throughout most of the Lushootseed speaking territory the word for *dog* is sqʷəbayʔ. However, among the Muckleshoot the word has become sqʷubayʔ.

3.6. Vocabulary comment. The words sčədadxʷ and sʔuladxʷ have been rendered in English as *salmon*. Although this is a convenient **gloss** (translation) and will be used throughout this reader, the student should know that *salmon* is not the exact meaning because included in the meaning of these Lushootseed words is the steelhead trout. The more precise English equivalent term is *anadromous fish*. However, this term is inappropriately technical for this reader. *Salmon* is used instead.

Note that both the Northern and Southern Lushootseed words end the same way, namely, -adxʷ, which is a suffix meaning *year*. Why is this ending appropriate in a word meaning salmon?

3.7. Homework. Look up the word *anadromous* in a large English dictionary. What does *ana-* mean? _____. What does *drom-* mean? _____.

3.8. Exercises. Translate the following sentences into Lushootseed:

   1. Did you folks roast a salmon?   _____.

   2. I took the dog in the house. _____.

   3. We looked for the girl. _____.

   4. The boy looked for [someone/something]. _____.

   5. Did [someone] roast the salmon?   _____.

   6. The girl went into the house.   _____.

   7. We took the dog home.   _____.

   8. [Someone] took [someone/something] somewhere.   _____.

   9. [She] brought the dog into the house. _____.

   10. We roasted the salmon. _____.

11. Did you look for the dog? _____.

12. Did [someone] bring the boy? _____.

LESSON FOUR

-s and -d, goal; experiencer

The student has learned two different suffixes which mark a verb as taking a patient noun, namely, -txʷ and -d. There are three more such suffixes in Lushootseed, two of which are presented in this lesson.

1a. ʔuʔusil ti c̓ix̌c̓ix̌.	The fish hawk dove.
1b. ʔuʔusis ti sʔuladxʷ.	[It] dove after the salmon.
2a. ʔutəlawil ti sqʷəbayʔ.	The dog ran.
2b. ʔutəlawis ti sqigʷac.	[It] ran after a deer.
3a. ʔuɫalil ti lux̌.	The old man went ashore.
3b. ʔuɫalis ti sup̓qs*.	[He] went ashore after a hair seal.
4a. ʔuɫčil* tsi č̓ač̓as.	The girl arrived.
4b. ʔuɫčis ti lux̌.	[She] arrived [to see/visit] the old man.

Do the nouns in these (a)-sentences express agents or patients? _____.
All verbs in the (a)-sentences end in what suffix? _____. For similarity in grammatical function should this suffix be matched with -b or with -txʷ and -d? _____.
Do the nouns in the (b)-sentences convey agents or patients? _____. All verbs in the (b)-sentences end in what suffix? _____. For similarity in grammatical functions, should this suffix be matched with -b or with -txʷ and -d? _____.

4.1. In the above example sentences, the formation of patient oriented verbs (i.e., those followed by nouns expressing patients) can be thought of in two ways. Students may either choose to say that -is replaces -il, or they may say that -s is added following -il and, when this happens, the 'l' of -il drops. (This grammar describes Lushootseed in terms of the second alternative.)

4.2. Optional. (The student may elect to omit this section.) There is another set of -il verbs which becomes patient oriented by the addition of -d instead of -s. For example, xʷit̓il means *fall off* while xʷit̓ild means *drop something*. Words like xʷit̓ild function in Lushootseed grammar just like gʷəč̓əd and other verbs in -d; therefore, students who only intend to read Lushootseed have nothing new to learn about these -il-d verbs.

13

Nevertheless, some will find it interesting to know why some verbs ending in -il become patient oriented by the addition of -s while others take -d. Study the following short sentences paying particular attention to the meaning of the verbs in the (a)-sentences:

5a. ʔuxʷit'il ti čʔačʔas.   The boy fell off.

5b. ʔuxʷit'ild ti čʔačʔas.   [Someone] knocked the boy off.

6a. ʔucłil ti sqigʷac.   The deer bled.

6b. ʔucłild ti sqigʷac.   [Someone] bled the deer.

7a. ʔuƛ'uxʷil ti sʔəłəd.   The food got cold.

7b. ʔuƛ'uxʷild ti sʔəłəd.   [Someone] cooled off the food.

8a. ʔuččil* ti čaləs*.   The hand(s) became red.

8b. ʔuččild ti čaləs.   [Someone] reddened the hand(s).

List the four verbs from the (a)-sentences 1 through 4 above in one column and those from this second set of (a)-sentences, 5 through 8, in an adjacent column. Beside each verb write its gloss.

1 through 4	English glosses	5 through 8	English glosses
_____	_____	_____	_____
_____	_____	_____	_____
_____	_____	_____	_____
_____	_____	_____	_____

4.2a. The words in the left column are all agent oriented, that is, the nouns associated with them express agents. However, the verbs in the right column are not agent oriented. The nouns associated with them convey **experiencers** rather than agents. Such nouns stand for someone who suffers or undergoes an event without design or intent or else simply endures a change in condition or state. Therefore, verbs on the right are said to be **experience oriented** or **experiencer verbs.**[3]

---

[3]Ultimately, of course, the experiencer is often responsible for the fate that befalls him/her, but the grammar of this set of verbs does not involve itself with matters of responsibility. See, however, the suffix -dxʷ in the next lesson.

4.2b. Note that the noun associated with an experiencer verb is not a patient. The term *patient* is used only when someone else does something to the person or thing the noun represents.

4.3. Similar to the suffix -s is -c. This suffix is illustrated in the third sentence in each of the following groups:

9a.	ʔuʔux̌ʷ tsi luχ.	The old woman went.
9b.	ʔuʔux̌ʷtxʷ tsi luχ.	[Someone] took the old woman somewhere.
9c.	ʔuʔux̌ʷc tsi luχ.	[Someone] went after the old woman.
10a.	ʔuʔəλ̕ ti sqʷəbayʔ.	The dog came.
10b.	ʔuʔəλ̕txʷ ti sqʷəbayʔ.	[Someone] brought the dog.
10c.	ʔuʔəλ̕c ti sqʷəbayʔ.	[Someone] came for the dog.
11a.	ʔučubə ti luχ.	The old man went inland.
11b.	ʔučubətxʷ* ti luχ.	[Someone] took/brought the old man inland.
11c.	ʔučubaac ti luχ.	[Someone] went/came inland after the old man.
12a.	ʔuhədʔiw̕ tsi luχ.	The old woman went/came in the house.
12b.	ʔuhədʔiw̕txʷ tsi luχ.	[Someone] took/brought the old woman into the house.
12c.	ʔuhədʔiw̕c tsi luχ.	[Someone] went/came into the house after the old woman.

The third sentence in each of these groups (9 through 12) exemplifies still another patient orienting suffix, namely -c. This suffix goes with fewer verbs than the others, but most of those verbs that do take -c are very common.

4.3a. When -c is added to a verb stem that ends in a vowel, that vowel is lengthened. Lengthened or **long vowels** are represented in Lushootseed writing by doubling the vowel letter.

4.3b. However, ə can never be long in Lushootseed. Where a long ə-vowel is expected (as in ʔučubə *went/came inland* followed by -c), a long a-vowel replaces it. Thus, ʔučubə + c becomes ʔučubaac.

4.4. With verbs expressing the movement of someone from one place to another, both -s and -c designate a **goal,** the purpose for the journey. (In Lushootseed **goal** may be thought of as a subtype of patient.) On the other hand, -txʷ is a **causative** suffix. For example, *bring* as expressed in Lushootseed is literally *cause to come*.

4.5. As with verbs ending in -txʷ and -d so too with those ending in -s and -c, čəd- words represent an agent.

13. ʔuɬalis čəd ti supʼqs.	I went ashore after the hair seal.
14. ʔuɬčis čəxʷ ʔu ti luχ.	Did you arrive to [visit] the old man?
15. ʔutəlawis čəɬ ti sqʷəbayʔ.	We ran after the dog.
16. ʔuʔux̌ʷc čələp ʔu tsi čačʼas.	Did you folks go after the girl?
17. ʔučubaac čəɬ ti sqigʷac.	We went inland after a deer.
18. ʔuʔəxʼc čəxʷ ʔu tsi luχ.	Did you come after the old woman?

4.6. Vocabulary comment. Usually a verb taking -txʷ does not also take -d, and most verbs ending in -b that designate movement to a place do not also occur with no ending at all. However, ʔuhədʔiwʼ- is such a verb. Thus, ʔuhədʔiwʼ and ʔuhədʔiwʼb are more or less synonomous expressions as are ʔuhədʔiwʼtxʷ and ʔuhədʔiwʼd.

ʔuhədʔiwʼ tsi luχ.	= ʔuhədʔiwʼb tsi luχ.	= The old woman entered the house.
ʔuhədʔiwʼtxʷ tsi luχ.	= ʔuhədʔiwʼd tsi luχ.	= [Someone] took/brought the old woman into the house.
ʔuhədʔiwʼc tsi luχ.		[Someone] went/came into the house after the old woman.

4.7. Dialect differences.

4.7a. Instead of ɬčil *arrive*, speakers of Southern Lushootseed use either ɬəčil or ɬəči (with stress on the first vowel in both cases). When one or more suffixes is added to ɬəči(l) however, everyone does pronounce the l -- except, of course, when that added ending is the goal suffix -s (4.1).

4.7b. Among the Snohomish the word for *hair seal* is supʼqs, but elsewhere, both to the north and south, the equivalent term is ʔasxʷ.

4.7c. In Southern Lushootseed the word for *hand* is čaləš rather than čaləs. This difference is exactly like that for čʼačʼaš versus čʼačʼas (1.4).

4.7d. ʔučcil *became red* in the north is matched by ʔukʷiXʼil in the south. Note, however, that a river in Northern Lushootseed territory bears a name clearly derived from the Southern Lushootseed word. This is the Pilchuk River called dxʷkʷiXʼəb in Lushootseed. (*Pilchuk* itself is from Chinook Jargon and means *red water*.) The fact that a Northern Lushootseed place name is derived from what is now a Southern Lushootseed word suggests what about the original territory in which the word was once spoken?

4.7e. Instead of ʔučubətxʷ *took/brought inland*, the oldest speaker of Lushootseed to have been recorded on tape in the 1950's said, ʔučubəstxʷ. A long time ago Lushootseed speakers used -stxʷ in place of -txʷ after verb stems ending in a vowel. Today only -txʷ is used regardless of the last sound of the verb stem.

4.8. Exercises. Translate the following into Lushootseed:

1. [Someone] took the old woman somewhere. _____ .

2. We went inland after a deer. _____ .

3. Did [someone] go after the dog? _____ .

4. Did the hair seal dive? _____ .

5. The dog ran. _____ .

6. I ran after the dog. _____ .

7. Did you bring it into the house? _____ .

8. Did you come after the old man? _____ .

9. We arrived [in time] for it. _____ .

The following sentences are the "bare bones" of a short sequence from an old story. Several words and suffixes yet to be studied have been omitted here. In this story čixčix *Fish Hawk* is a person. Render these lines in English.

1. ʔuʔusil ti čixčix. _____ .

2. ʔuʔusis ti sʔuladxʷ. _____ .

3. ʔučubətxʷ. _____ .

4. ʔutʼukʷtxʷ. _____ .

LESSON FIVE

-dxʷ; summary of patient oriented suffixes

Presented in this lesson is the fifth patient suffix, -dxʷ. In addition to its purely grammatical function of providing for a following patient noun, it has an added significance that separates it from the other two patient suffixes -- especially from -d. Study the following pairs of sentences and their translations. In what way does this new suffix, -dxʷ, differ from -d?

1a.	ʔukʷ"əɬəd ti qʷuʔ.	[Someone] poured the water.
1b.	ʔukʷ"əɬdxʷ ti qʷuʔ.	[Someone] spilled the water.
2a.	ʔubəčad* ti čačas.	[Someone] put the boy down.
2b.	ʔubəčdxʷ ti čačas.	[Someone] happened to knock the boy over.
3a.	ʔukʷədad* ti sqʷəbayʔ.	[Someone] took a hold of the dog.
3b.	ʔukʷəd(d)xʷ ti sqʷəbayʔ.	[Someone] managed to get a hold of the dog.
4a.	ʔucʼəld ti luX.	[Someone] defeated/got the better of the old man.
4b.	ʔucʼəldxʷ ti luX.	[Someone] managed to defeat/get the better of the old man.

5.1. In sentences 1b and 2b the act is performed inadvertently, accidentally; while in 3b and 4b the act is done deliberately but with difficulty. Nevertheless, both types of actions are indicated in Lushootseed with the same suffix, -dxʷ. Obviously, the way Lushootseed speakers view these events is different from the way English speakers do.

Before reading further, the student should pause for a minute or two to ponder what *to do accidentally* shares in meaning with *to accomplish only with difficulty*.

The common concept is **lack of (full) control over the outcome.** In all sentences, (a) and (b), someone is clearly responsible for what happened (even though that someone is often not explicitly stated in the Lushootseed sentence as is the case in these examples); but in the (b)-sentences the person responsible is not really master of the situation, while in the (a)-sentences the one responsible is also assumed to be in control of events. Degree of control permeates the Lushootseed verbal system.

18

Whether the student translates sentences with verbs ending in -dxʷ using *accidentally* and the like or by using *accomplish with difficulty* depends upon the context and the type of action and agents involved. The appropriate translation is seldom a problem once the basic meaning of -dxʷ is understood.

5.2. This suffix -dxʷ is usually pronounced as though it were spelled -ədxʷ. However, the ə-vowel is not included in the standard spelling of this suffix.

5.3. A few verb stems rarely occur with any suffix other than -dxʷ because their very meaning implies less than full control. One such is the Lushootseed word for *find*.

ʔuʔəy'dxʷ[4] čəd tsi čʼačʼas.	I found the girl.
ʔuʔəy'dxʷ ti sqʷʼəbayʔ.	[Someone] found the dog.

(See also 10.6.)

5.4. The student has now learned five suffixes which mark a verb as being patient oriented. With a few minor exceptions these five comprise the complete set of patient suffixes. They are summarised here.

-txʷ	*causative*	With stems referring to travel, -txʷ is often glossed with take/bring.
-s	*goal*	This suffix is found only with verb stems in -il (and -il + -s becomes -is.)
-c	*goal*	This suffix occurs with a relatively small number of verb stems. It has the meaning *goal* only with a subset of those, namely, the ones describing travel of some sort, but it never follows stems in -il. With other sorts of stems yet to be presented, -c has more abstract and less specifiable glosses beyond that of simply patient marker.
-dxʷ	*lack of control*	In general, any verb stem taking -d can have -dxʷ instead. (Other nuances are expressed by -dxʷ when following certain verb stems to be presented later.)

---

[4]Most speakers pronounce this word as though it were spelled ʔuʔiʔdxʷ.

-d   This patient suffix can be added to the greatest variety of verb stems. It cannot be glossed more specifically than its general patient stem-forming significance. In the lessons up to this point, -d has been presented in contrast to -b and with experiential verbs in -il.

5.5 Dialect differences.

5.5a. The Skagit say ʔuɬaq'ad and ʔuɬaq'dxʷ instead of ʔubəčad and ʔubəčdxʷ.

5.5b. In Southern Lushootseed many speakers pronounce ʔubəčad and ʔukʷədad as though they were spelled ʔubəčəd and ʔukʷədəd.

5.6 Exercises. On a separate sheet of paper, translate the following sentences into Lushootseed:

    1. Did you manage to defeat the people? (*People* is ʔaciɬtalbixʷ.)

    2. [Someone] put the girl down.

    3. Did you spill the water?

    4. We arrived to [visit] the old woman.

    5. Did you folks go ashore after the boy?

    6. We ran after the dog.

    7. Did you folks cook the salmon?

    8. Did you find the dog?

On a separate sheet of paper, translate the following into English:

    1. ʔuʔəy'dxʷ čəxʷ ʔu ti sqʷəbayʔ.

    2. ʔuʔux̌ʷc čəd ti sqigʷac.

    3. ʔučubaac ʔu ti č'ač'as.

    4. ʔubəčdxʷ čəxʷ ʔu ti luX̌.

    5. ʔukʷʼəɬəd čəd ti qʷuʔ.

    6. ʔuc'əldxʷ čəxʷ ʔu.

    7. ʔukʷədad ti č'ač'as.

8. ʔukʷəd(d)xʷ čəxʷ ʔu ti sʔuladxʷ.

9. ʔubəčad čəɬ tsi luX̌.

10. ʔuʔəy'dxʷ tsi luX̌.

Fill in the blanks following the words of each set with the appropriate glosses. Some of these verbs are entirely new but the student will find most glosses to be obvious. A few, however, will require a little imagination because what English speakers assume to be the basic meaning of a verb stem on the basis of that stem with one suffix sometimes turns out not to fit when that same stem occurs with a different suffix. For example, consider ʔučalad and ʔučaltxʷ below.

ʔuɬalil went ashore	ʔuqəɬ woke up	ʔukʷədad took smth.
ʔuɬalis _____	ʔuqəɬəd _____	ʔukʷəd(d)xʷ _____
ʔuɬalildxʷ _____	ʔuqəɬdxʷ _____	
ʔuɬaliltxʷ _____		

	ʔubəč fell over	ʔusaqʷ flew
ʔučalad chased someone	ʔubəčad _____	
ʔučaldxʷ _____	ʔubəčdxʷ _____	
ʔučaltxʷ caught someone		ʔusaqʷtxʷ _____

ʔuɬčil arrived	ʔutədʸil went to bed	ʔux̌ʷsil grew fat
ʔuɬčis _____	ʔutədʸis _____	ʔux̌ʷsild _____
ʔuɬčildxʷ _____		
ʔuɬčiltxʷ _____	ʔutədʸiltxʷ _____	

LESSON SIX

Patient suffixes + b, ʔə + agent

Compare the following sentences with each other and with their English translations. Then answer the questions below.

1a.	ʔuʔusil ti čixčiǰ.	The fish hawk dove.
1b.	ʔuʔusis ti sʔuladxʷ.	[It] dove after a salmon.
1c.	ʔuʔusisəb ʔə ti čixčiǰ ti sʔuladxʷ.	The fish hawk dove after a salmon.
2a.	ʔuʔuǰʷ ti luǰ.	The old man went.
2b.	ʔuʔuǰʷc ti čačas.	[He] went after the boy.
2c.	ʔuʔuǰʷcəb ʔə ti luǰ ti čačas.	The old man went after the boy.
3a.	ʔuʔuǰʷ ti luǰ.	The old man went.
3b.	ʔuʔuǰʷtxʷ ti čačas.	[He] took the boy somewhere.
3c.	ʔuʔuǰʷtub ʔə ti luǰ ti čačas.	The old man took the boy somewhere.
4a.	0	
4b.	ʔuʔəy'dxʷ ti sqʷəbayʔ.	[Someone] found the dog.
4c.	ʔuʔəy'dub ʔə ti čačas ti sqʷəbayʔ.	The boy found the dog.
4d.	ʔuʔəy'dub ʔə ti sqʷəbayʔ ti čačas.	The dog found the boy.
5a.	0	
5b.	ʔukʷədad ti sqʷəbayʔ.	[Someone] took a hold of the dog.
5c.	ʔukʷədatəb ʔə tsi čačas ti sqʷəbayʔ.	The girl took a hold of the dog.

Each (a)-sentence has how many nouns? _____. How many nouns are there in each (b)-sentence? _____. In the (c)-sentences, does the first noun following the particle ʔə stand for an agent or a patient? _____. What does the other noun in the (c)-sentences represent? _____. What suffix do all verbs in the (c)-sentences share that is lacking in all the (b)-sentences? _____. What seems to be the function (purpose) of this new suffix? _____.

6.1. Three of the suffixes in the (b)-sentences above are seen to have two forms. When final in a word, they are said one way; but when followed by the suffix -b, they are pronounced differently. Similarly, -b is pronounced one way when following a vowel but another when coming after a consonant.

Final	Before -b	Patient suffix + -b
-s	-s-	-s-əb
-c	-c-	-c-əb
-txʷ	-tu-	-tu-b
-dxʷ	-du-	-du-b
-d	-t-	-t-əb

6.2. Two nouns, one for agent and the other for patient, can follow the same verb when that verb bears the suffix sequence **patient suffix + -b.** This -b is not to be confused with the agent suffix -b of words like gʷəč'əb (first presented in Lesson Three).

6.3. As with other verb stems, so too with those having a patient suffix + -b, either the agent or the patient or both may be omitted.

ʔuʔusisəb ʔə ti c'ixčix ti sʔuladxʷ.	The fish hawk dove after the salmon.
ʔuʔusisəb ti sʔuladxʷ.	[Something] dove after the salmon.
ʔuʔusisəb ʔə ti c'ixčix.	The fish hawk dove after [something].
ʔuʔusisəb.	[Something] dove after [something].
ʔukʷədatəb ʔə tsi čač̓as ti sqʷəbayʔ.	The girl took a hold of the dog.
ʔukʷədatəb ti sqʷəbayʔ.	[Someone] took a hold of the dog.
ʔukʷədatəb ʔə tsi čač̓as.	The girl took a hold of [something].
ʔukʷədatəb.	[Someone] took a hold of [something].

The following eight sentences show clearly the importance of ʔə. Read through these sentences and answer the questions immediately below.

6a.	ʔugʷəč'təb ʔə ti čač̓as ti sqʷəbayʔ.	The boy looked for the dog.
6b.	ʔugʷəč'təb ti sqʷəbayʔ ʔə ti čač̓as.	The boy looked for the dog.
7a.	ʔugʷəč'təb ʔə ti sqʷəbayʔ ti čač̓as.	The dog looked for the boy.
7b.	ʔugʷəč'təb ti čač̓as ʔə ti sqʷəbayʔ.	The dog looked for the boy.
8a.	ʔut'ukʷtub ʔə ti čač̓as tsi čač̓as.	The boy took the girl home.
8b.	ʔut'ukʷtub tsi čač̓as ʔə ti čač̓as.	The boy took the girl home.
9a.	ʔut'ukʷtub ʔə tsi čač̓as ti čač̓as.	The girl took the boy home.
9b.	ʔut'ukʷtub ti čač̓as ʔə tsi čač̓as.	The girl took the boy home.

What is the function (purpose) of ʔə in these sentences? _____
_____. Without ʔə would it always be possible to
distinguish agent from patient? _____.

6.4. In spite of this variable order between agent and patient nouns, by far the most
common arrangement is for the agent noun to precede the patient noun. Therefore, when
writing or speaking, students should place the agent noun ahead of the patient noun (unless
specifically told to do otherwise), but they should also be alert to the other possible
arrangement when encountered in these texts.

6.5. The čəd-words always come before nouns.

    10. ʔutʼukʷtub čəxʷ ʔu ʔə ti luχ.   Did the old man take you home?

    11. ʔutəlawisəb čəd ʔə ti sqʷəbayʔ.   The dog ran after me.

    12. ʔugʷəčʼtəb[5] čəɬ ʔə ti sqʷəbayʔ.   The dog looked for us.

    13. ʔuʔəyʼdub čələp ʔu ʔə tsi čačas.   Did the girl find you folks?

    14. ʔuʔəƛʼcəb čəxʷ ʔu ʔə ti ʔaciɬtalbixʷ.   Did the people come for/after you?

Following the sequence patient suffix + -b, do čəd-words express the agent or the patient?
_____. Where does the interrogative particle, ʔu, occur in the sentence
relative to the čəd-words? _____. Where does it occur
relative to the particle ʔə? _____.

6.6. Dialect differences. The Swinomish and the people living along the Skagit River
pronounce ʔaciɬtalbixʷ *people* as though it were spelled ʔaciɬtəbixʷ.

6.7. Exercises. On a separate sheet of paper rewrite the following sentences by changing
the patient into the agent and the agent into the patient. Then translate the new sentences.

    1. ʔuʔəyʼdub ʔə ti čačas ti sqʷəbayʔ.

    2. ʔutəlawisəb ʔə ti sqʷəbayʔ ti luχ.

    3. ʔuhədʔiwʼcəb ʔə ti čačas tsi čačas.

    4. ʔugʷəčʼtəb ʔə tsi luχ tsi čačas.

    5. ʔuʔəƛʼtub ʔə ti ʔaciɬtalbixʷ ti luχ.

---

[5]The second ə̱ in ʔugʷəčʼəd disappears before the sequence -t-əb.

As above, rewrite the following sentences so that the original agent is now patient and the original patient is now agent. Then translate the resulting sentences into English. (It may be necessary to review Lesson Two at this point.)

1. ʔutʼukʷtub čəxʷ ʔu ʔə tsi luχ.

2. ʔuʔəyʼdub čəd ʔə ti čʼačʼas.

3. ʔuɬčisəb čəɬ ʔə ti ʔaciɬtalbixʷ.

4. ʔučubaacəb čələp ʔu ʔə ti luχ.

5. ʔubəčatəb čəxʷ ʔu ʔə tsi luχ.

LESSON SEVEN

Agent oriented stems, ʔə + patient

7.1. Agent oriented stems divide into two subclasses, those that directly involve only one entity, the agent, and those that not only involve an agent but also imply a patient.

7.1a. It is not possible to distinguish the two types by simply looking at them. Only their meanings betray their different subclass membership. For example, ʔusaxʷəb *jumped/ran* and ʔugʷəč'əb *searched* have the same form -- the same number of consonants and vowels in the same relative order and they both end in -b, but ʔugʷəč'əb implies the person or thing sought as well as the seeker whereas ʔusaxʷəb involves only the jumper/runner.

7.1b. The implied patient of verbs like ʔugʷəč'əb, ʔuqʷʷəlb, etc., can be expressed overtly by means of an ʔə-phrase.

1. ʔugʷəč'əb ti č'ač'as <u>ʔə</u> <u>ti</u> <u>sqələlalitut</u>.   The boy quested for spirit power.
2. ʔuqʷʷəlb tsi luX <u>ʔə</u> <u>ti</u> <u>sʔuladxʷ</u>.   The old woman roasted a salmon.
3. ʔuhədʔiw'b ti luX <u>ʔə</u> <u>ti</u> <u>hud</u>.   The old man brought the wood inside.
4. ʔugʷəč'əb čəd <u>ʔə</u> <u>ti</u> <u>sqələlalitut</u>.   I quested for spirit power.
5. ʔuqʷʷəlb čəd <u>ʔə</u> <u>ti</u> <u>sʔuladxʷ</u>.   I roasted a salmon.
6. ʔuhədʔiw'b čəd <u>ʔə</u> <u>ti</u> <u>hud</u>.   I brought the wood inside.

7.1c. In Lesson Six it was learned that a noun expressing an agent could be added to sentences with patient oriented verbs (with appropriate changes of verb suffixes). Now it is seen that a noun expressing a patient can be added to a sentence having an agent oriented verb of the second type (7.1) and without a change in suffix. In both cases the 'added' noun is preceded by ʔə regardless of whether the addition is serving as agent or patient.

Therefore, students must be particularly careful to distinguish sentences with agent oriented verb stems having a <u>patient introduced by ʔə</u> as in 7.1b from sentences with patient oriented stems having an <u>agent introduced by ʔə</u> as in Lesson Six. This distinction is partiulary important when both nouns represent living beings which logically can serve either the agent or patient role.

7a. ʔugʷəč'əb ti čačas ʔə tsi čačas.   The boy looked for the girl.

7b. ʔugʷəč'təb ʔə ti čačas tsi čačas.   The boy looked for the girl.

Although ʔə-phrase agents expressed by nouns usually precede patients, this order can be switched (6.4).

7c. ʔugʷəč'təb tsi čačas ʔə ti čačas.   The boy looked for the girl.

This last arrangement looks even more like example sentence 7a than does 7b because both ʔə-phrases are now in final position. **It is crucial that students pay close attention to verb suffixes.**

7.2.   As with any and all Lushootseed verbs, so too with these discussed in 7.1 - 7.1c,   either the noun expressing the agent or the one conveying the patient, or both, can be omitted.   In other words, even the agent of an agent oriented verb can be omitted if the speaker so chooses as in 2b and 2d below.

2a. ʔuqʷəlb tsi luX ʔə ti sʔuladxʷ.   The old woman roasted a salmon.

2b. ʔuqʷəlb ʔə ti sʔuladxʷ.   [Someone] roasted a salmon.

2c. ʔuqʷəlb tsi luX.   The old woman roasted [something].

2d. ʔuqʷəlb.   [Someone] roasted [something].

7.3.   Thus far only three verbs have been learned that belong to this subclass of agent oriented verb stems.   Each of these ends in -b.   However, membership in this class is not limited to verbs with the -b suffix.   In addition to -b there are -alikʷ, -alc, a few verbs in -il, some with no suffix at all, and even one very common verb ending in -d (-- not the same -d, however, as occurs with patient oriented verbs).   Conversely, there exist verbs with final -b (along with -il and -alikʷ) that do not belong to this subclass.   An example is ʔusaxʷəb *jumped, ran* as mentioned above (7.1a).   It is an agent oriented verb like ʔuʔuxʷ *went* and ʔuʔəX' *came* and like others of this type, it can be turned into a patient oriented verb by the addition of -txʷ (or -tu-b), e.g., ʔusaxʷəbtxʷ *kidnapped [someone], caused [someone] to jump, run.*

Several examples of this subclass that do not end in -b are given here:

8a. ʔupusil ti čačas.   The boy was throwing[6] (as in a game, exercising, or simply passing time).

8b. ʔupusil ti čačas ʔə ti čX̌aʔ*.   The boy was throwing the stone.

9a. ʔušabalikʷ tsi luX̌.   The old woman dried [things].

9b. ʔušabalikʷ tsi luX̌ ʔə ti sʔuladxʷ.   The old woman dried salmon.

10a. ʔuhuyalc ti luX̌.   The old man finished [it].

10b. ʔuhuyalc ti luX̌ ʔə ti ʔalʔal.   The old man finished the house.

11a. ʔuʔuləx̌ ti ʔaciɬtalbixʷ.   The people gathered [things].

11b. ʔuʔuləx̌ ti ʔaciɬtalbixʷ ʔə ti bəsqʷ.   The people gathered crab.

12a. ʔuʔəɬəd tsi čačas.   The girl ate.

12b. ʔuʔəɬəd tsi čačas ʔə ti bəsqʷ.   The girl ate crab.

7.4. Because the same verb root often occurs in bothpatient and agent stems, sentences with verbs of one orientation are obviously synonymous with those of the other (when both agent and patient are included). Consider the following pairs:

13a. ʔušabatəb ʔə tsi luX̌ ti sʔuladxʷ.   The old woman dried the salmon.

13b. ʔušabalikʷ tsi luX̌ ʔə ti sʔuladxʷ.   The old woman dried the salmon.

14a. ʔugʷəč'təb ʔə ti čačas ti sqʷəbayʔ.   The boy looked for the dog.

14b. ʔugʷəč'əb ti čačas ʔə ti sqəlalitut.   The boy quested for a guardian spirit.

15a. ʔuʔuləx̌təb ʔə ti luX̌ tihud.   The old man kept the wood [which he happened to come upon].

15b. ʔuʔuləx̌ ti luX̌ ʔə ti bəsqʷ.   The old man foraged for crab.

16a. ʔuč'aʔtəb ʔə tsi luX̌ ti skʷiʔxʷ.   The old woman dug up braken fern rhizome(s).[7]

16b. ʔuč'aʔəb tsi luX̌ ʔə ti skʷiʔxʷ.   The old woman dug braken fern rhizomes (as in 'harvesting' from nature).

---

[6]The student will note that the English translations of example sentences 8a and 8b use the so called past progressive, *was throwing*, instead of the simple past, *threw*. These could, in fact, be translated either way. Lushootseed grammar does not always require a distinction between the simple and the progressive where English does.

[7]A *rhizome* is technically a stem but one that grows under (or along) the ground. The Lushootseed roasted and ate braken fern rhizomes for their starch.

To say that these sentences are synonymous, however, is not to say that they are identical. In the (a)-sentences an agent does something to the patient -- the patient is of central importance. In the (b)-sentences, on the other hand, attention centers on the agent's activity which is typically performed with his/her own ends paramount. For many of this later type, especially those with verbs ending in -b, the patient is a product of some sort, something made, prepared, or otherwise produced. In technical parlance, verbs of the (a)-sentences are said to be in the **active voice** while those in the (b)-sentences are in the **middle voice.**

7.5. Optional. (The student may elect to omit this section.)

7.5a. Sometimes the patient permitted by an agent oriented verb is different from the possible patient of a patient oriented verb even though both verbs are built upon the same root. In 17a below only someone or something serving as target can be the patient, while in 17b only something thrown can be the patient. (Similar differences obtain with other verbs in -il.)

17a. Ɂupusutəb Ɂə ti čačas ti sqʷəbayɁ. The boy threw [something] at the dog.

17b. Ɂupusil ti čačas Ɂə ti čƛ̉aɁ. The boy was throwing a stone. [See fuller gloss at 8a above.]

18a. Ɂut̉uc̉utəb Ɂə ti luƛ ti sčətxʷəd.* The old man shot (at) the bear.

18b. Ɂut̉uc̉il ti luƛ Ɂə ti t̉isəd. The old man shot the arrow.

7.6. While many roots can serve in both agent and patient verbs, a few are limited to one or the other orientation. Such limited roots are often paired with a different root of similar meaning belonging to the other orientation. Sentence examples 19a and 19b illustrate the most common pair.

19a. Ɂuləkʷtəb* Ɂə tsi čačas ti bəsqʷ. The girl ate crab.

19b. ɁuɁəɫəd tsi čačas Ɂə ti bəsqʷ. The girl ate crab.

Students should **note with special care** the verb ɁuɁəɫəd *ate.* In its general form and final sound it seems to be the same as a patient oriented verb such as Ɂukʷəɫəd *poured.* In spite of this similarity, however, ɁuɁəɫəd **is an agent oriented verb.**

7.7. Dialect differences.

7.7a. The Southern Lushootseed equivalent to čƛ̉aɁ *rock, stone* is čəƛ̉əɁ.

7.7b. At Swinomish the word spaʔc is used for *black bear*, but at Sauk-Suiattle and throughout the rest of the Lushootseed speaking region the word is sčətxʷəd. (Note that the referent of these words does not include *grizzly bear*.)

7.7c. In place of ʔuləkʷ"əd *eat [something], put [something] in one's mouth*, the Swinomish and people living along the Skagit River say ʔuhuydxʷ.

7.8. Vocabulary comment. The word sqəlalitut has been glossed (translated) into English in this lesson as *guardian spirit*. The concept does not exist in modern Anglo culture, but the ideas that lie behind it are fundamental to the Lushootseed view of the world. Several of the texts in this reader are directly concerned with sqəlalitut and a full comprehension of most others depends upon an understanding of the guardian spirit. Interested readers should see page 497 in volume 7 of the *Handbook of North American Indians* referred to in the introduction to this reader.

7.9. Exercises. The following sentences of the first set all have patient oriented verbs. Provide an appropriate gloss for each of these. Then on a separate sheet of paper recast each sentence using the corresponding agent oriented verb and gloss the new sentence as well. (In number 3 it will also be necessary to change the patient selecting one that is more appropriate with the altered verb because one does not ordinarily throw dogs.)

1. ʔušabatəb ʔə tsi luX ti sʔuladxʷ.
2. ʔugʷəč'təb ʔə ti ʔaciłtalbixʷ ti sqəlalitut.
3. ʔupusutəb ʔə ti čačas ti sqʷəbayʔ.
4. ʔuləkʷ"təb ʔə ti sqʷəbayʔ ti bəsqʷ.

The next four sentences all have agent oriented verbs. On a separate sheet of paper give an appropriate gloss for each and recast these using a patient oriented verb in each. Then render the new sentence in English.

5. ʔuʔuləX ti luX ʔə ti hud.
6. ʔuč'aʔəb tsi čačas ʔə ti skʷiʔxʷ.
7. ʔuʔəłəd ti čačas ʔə ti bəsqʷ.
8. ʔuqʷ"əlb tsi luX ʔə ti sʔuladxʷ.

In the final set of sentences immediately below students are to underline the patient in each sentence that has one. Much of the vocabulary has not been presented before and most of these new words are not in the glossary at the back of this reader either. The grammar, however, is all familiar. Students are expected to rely on the grammar, particularly the verb endings, to identify the patient nouns.

1. ʔucʼəldub ti sčətxʷəd ʔə ti čixčix̌.

2. ʔuyiqʼib tsi sɬadəyʔ ʔə ti spču.ʔ.

3. ʔuyiqʼitəb ʔə tsi sɬadəyʔ ti spču.ʔ.

4. ʔucʼəlalikʷ tsi x̌ax̌acʼapəd.

5. ʔuyiqʼid ti spču.ʔ.

6. ʔupusil ti ləgʷəb.

7. ʔuyəcəb ti stubš ʔə ti syəcəb.

8. ʔuɬičʼib ʔə ti ʔulal.

9. ʔupusutəb ʔə ti čʼačʼas ti sbiaw.

10. ʔupusil ʔə ti čʼx̌aʔ.

11. ʔuʔəɬəd ti qʷist ʔə ti sqʷiʔqʷaliʔ.

12. ʔupusil ti čʼačʼas ʔə ti čʼx̌a.

SUMMARY OF FUNCTION MARKING

Terms such as *agent, patient* (including *goal* 4.4), and *experiencer* (4.2a) are collectively referred to as **roles**. Roles identify the various functions a noun or čəd-word has in the sentence. In English these roles are primarily signalled by word order and prepositions, but verb suffixes and ʔə convey these roles in Lushootseed.

In English the roles of nouns and pronouns are expressed identically. The student should remember, however, that in Lushootseed the roles of nouns and čəd-words are **not** always conveyed the same way. Specifically, a čəd-word with a verb ending in one of the patient suffixes stands for the agent while a noun following a patient suffix expresses a patient.

The following lists summarize the roles and their indicators that have been presented to this point:

I. Agent Oriented Stems
(Both the noun and the čəd-word express agents.)

ʔuʔux̌ʷ tsi č'ač'as.	The girl went.	ʔuʔux̌ʷ čəd.	I went.
ʔuʔusil ti č'ač'as.	The boy dove.	ʔuʔusil čəd.	I dove.
ʔusax̌ʷəb ti č'ač'as.	The boy jumped/ran.	ʔusax̌ʷəb čəd.	I jumped/ran.

II. Middle Voice Stems
(Both the noun and the čəd-word express agents. A second noun introduced by ʔə expresses patient.)

ʔugʷəč'əb ti luх̌ ʔə ti sqəlalitut.	ʔugʷəč'əb čəd ʔə ti sqəlalitut.
The old man quested for a guardian spirit.	I quested for a guardian spirit.
ʔuqʷʷəlb tsi luх̌ ʔə ti sʔuladxʷ.	ʔuqʷʷəlb čəd ʔə ti sʔuladxʷ.
The old woman roasted the salmon.	I roasted the salmon.
ʔuʔəɫəd ti ʔaciɫtalbix ʔə ti sʔuladxʷ.	ʔuʔəɫəd čəd ʔə ti sʔuladxʷ.
The people ate the salmon.	I ate the salmon.

III. Patient/Goal Oriented Stems
(The noun represents a patient (or goal) but the čəd-word is agent.)

ʔuʔux̌ʷtx̌ʷ tsi č'ač'as.	[Someone] took the girl somewhere.	ʔuʔux̌ʷtx̌ʷ čəd.	I took [her] somewhere.
ʔuʔux̌ʷc tsi č'ač'as.	[Smn] went after the girl.	ʔuʔux̌ʷc čəd.	I went after [her].
ʔuʔusis ti č'ač'as.	[Smn] dove after the boy.	ʔuʔusis čəd.	I dove after [him].
ʔugʷəč'əd tsi č'ač'as.	[Smn] sought the girl.	ʔugʷəč'əd čəd.	I sought [her].
ʔuʔəy'dx̌ʷ ti č'ač'as.	[Smn] found the boy.	ʔuʔəy'dx̌ʷ čəd.	I found [him].

IV. Passive Stems (a subtype of Patient/Goal Stems)
(The noun and čəd-word are both patient. Nouns going with ʔə are agent.)

ʔuʔux̌ʷtub ʔə ti č'ač'as tsi č'ač'as.
The boy took the girl (somewhere).

ʔuʔux̌ʷtub čəd ʔə ti č'ač'as.
The boy took me (somewhere.)

ʔuʔux̌ʷcəb ʔə ti č'ač'as tsi č'ač'as.
The boy went after the girl.

ʔuʔux̌ʷcəb čəd ʔə ti č'ač'as.
The boy went after me.

ʔuʔusisəb ʔə ti c'ix̌c'ix̌ ti sʔuladx̌ʷ.
The fish hawk dove after the salmon.

ʔuʔusisəb čəd ʔə ti č'ač'as.
The boy dove after me.

ʔugʷəč'təb ʔə ti č'ač'as tsi č'ač'as.
The boy looked for the girl.

ʔugʷəč'təb čəd ʔə ti č'ač'as.
The boy looked for me.

ʔuʔəy'dub ʔə ti č'ač'as tsi č'ač'as.
The boy found the girl.

ʔuʔəy'dub čəd ʔə ti č'ač'as.
The boy found me.

V. Experiencer Oriented Stems
(The noun and čəd-word are both experiencer.)

ʔux̌ʷit'il ti č'ač'as.	The boy fell off.	ʔux̌ʷit'il čəd.	I fell off.
ʔubəč ti č'ač'as.	The boy fell over.	ʔubəč čəd.	I fell over.

LESSON EIGHT

-yi- role, ʔə + recipient

Review page three. Then compare the following four sentences with one another and answer the questions below.

1. ʔuʔux̌ʷ ti č̓ač̓as.   The boy went.

2. ʔuʔux̌ʷyid* ti č̓ač̓as.   [Someone] went instead of the boy. (Someone went so he wouldn't have to.)

3. ʔuʔux̌ʷtx̌ʷ ti č̓ač̓as.   [Someone] took the boy somewhere.

4. ʔuʔux̌ʷtx̌ʷyid ti č̓ač̓as.   [Someone] took [something/someone] somewhere for the boy.

Describe how the role (function) of ti č̓ač̓as in sentence 2 differs from the role of ti č̓ač̓as in sentence 3.

_____

_____

_____

Is the role of ti č̓ač̓as in sentence 2 approximately the same as in sentence 4 or are their functions entirely different? _____.

What is the name of the role of ti č̓ač̓as in sentence 1? _____.

What is the name of the role of ti č̓ač̓as in sentence 3? _____.

8.1. There are at least five terms in linguistics used to convey the role of ti č̓ač̓as in sentences 2 and 4 above. These are *benefactive, dative, indirect object, recipient,* and *second object.* None of these is fully satisfactory for Lushootseed. Therefore, in Lushootseed grammar one simply speaks of the **-yi-role.** (In Southern Lushootseed the equivalent term is the -ši-role. See 8.5.)

8.2. Five roles have now been presented. These are agent, experiencer, patient, goal and -yi-role. Of these, only the patient and goal can be inanimate -- a thing -- although both are often animate. The others must be animate by the nature of what they represent in the real world.

When speakers use the -yi-role, both an agent and a patient (or goal) are either implied or specifically stated. In the following example sentences note carefully how these roles are distinguished. Also observe the variety of English prepositions that are used to convey the meaning of -yi-when it is suffixed to various verbs.

5a. ʔukʷədyid tsi čačas. [Someone] took [something] from the girl.
5b. ʔukʷədyid ʔə tiłaʔx̌. [Someone] took the platter [from someone].
5c. ʔukʷədyitəb ʔə tsi luX. The old woman took [something from someone].

6a. ʔuʔabyid ti sqʷəbayʔ. [Someone] gave [something] to the dog.
6b. ʔuʔabyid ʔə ti šaw̓. [Someone] gave a bone [to someone].
6c. ʔuʔabyitəb ʔə ti čačas. The boy gave [something to someone].

7a. ʔuʔux̌ʷtxʷyid ti čačas. [Someone] took [something] somewhere for the boy.
7b. ʔuʔux̌ʷtxʷyid ʔə ti sqʷəbayʔ. [Someone] took the dog somewhere [for someone].
7c. ʔuʔux̌ʷtxʷyitəb ʔə ti luX. The old man took [something/someone] somewhere for someone.

8a. ʔuʔəy'dxʷyid ti čačas. [Someone] found [something] for the boy.
8b. ʔuʔəy'dxʷyid ʔə ti sqʷəbayʔ. [Someone] found the dog [for someone].
8c. ʔuʔəy'dxʷyitəb ʔə tsi luX. The old woman found [something for someone].

8.2a. In sentences with -yi-how are patient and -yi-role distinguished? _____

_____.

8.2b. How are patient and agent distinguished in sentences with -yi-? _____

_____.

8.3. The example sentences above have only one noun per sentence. In 9 - 11 below there are two nouns, hence two roles expressed, in each sentence.

9. ʔuʔabyitəb ʔə ti luX ʔə ti sqʷəbayʔ. The old man gave [someone] a dog.
10. ʔuʔabyitəb ʔə ti luX ti čačas. The old man gave [something] to the boy.
11. ʔuʔabyitəb ti čačas ʔə ti sqʷəbayʔ. [Someone] gave the dog to the boy.

8.3a. What are the roles of the two nouns in sentence 9 and in which order do they occur?

_____

_____ .

8.3b. What are the roles and relative order of the two nouns in sentence 10? _____

_____ .

8.3c. What are the roles and relative order of the two nouns in sentence 11? _____

_____ .

8.3d. From the example sentences 9 - 11 one might expect to be able to include agent, patient (or goal), and -yi-role all with one verb. Nevertheless, Lushootseed grammar does not permit such sentences when all these roles would be represented by nouns. Speakers use any two but not three at once. (See, however, 20.5.)

8.4. On the other hand, with čəd-words (and another class of person markers to be presented in Lesson Nine), it is possible to have three roles with one verb.

12a. ʔuʔabyid čad ti čʼačʼas ʔə ti sqʷəbayʔ.	I gave the dog to the boy.
12b. ʔuʔabyid ti čʼačʼas ʔə ti sqʷəbayʔ.	[Someone] gave the dog to the boy.
12c. ʔuʔabyitəb čad ʔə ti čʼačʼas ʔə ti sqʷəbayʔ.	The boy gave me the dog.
13a. ʔukʷədyid čəxʷ ʔu tsi čʼačʼas ʔə ti kʷatʼaq.	Did you take the mat away from the girl?
13b. ʔukʷədyid tsi čʼačʼas ʔə ti kʷatʼaq.	[Someone] took the mat away from the girl.
13c. ʔukʷədyitəb čad ʔə tsi čʼačʼas ʔə ti kʷatʼaq.	The girl took the mat from me.
14a. ʔuləkʷʷyid čad ti luX̌ ʔə ti sʔuladxʷ.	I ate the old man['s] salmon. [Lit.: I ate the salmon away from the old man.]
14b. ʔuləkʷʷyid ti luX̌ ʔə ti sʔuladxʷ.	[Someone] ate the old man['s] salmon.
14c. ʔuləkʷʷyitəb čad ʔə ti luX̌ ʔə ti sʔuladxʷ.	The old man ate [my] salmon. (Lit.: The salmon was eaten [away] from me by the old man.)

8.5. Dialect differences. The suffix -yi- in Northern Lushootseed is equivalent to -ši- in Southern Lushootseed.   See 8.1.

8.6. Exercises. Translate the following sentences into Lushootseed:

   1. I took the bone from the dog. _____.

   2. The old man ate someone's salmon. _____.

   3. Someone came instead of the boy. _____.

   4. The girl brought something for the old woman. _____.

   5. Did you folks find the dog for the man? _____.

UNIT TWO

INFLECTION AND CLITICS

LESSON NINE

Person patient suffixes including the reflexive and reciprocal

9.1. There are several ways of expressing *me, us,* and *you* in Lushootseed. One of these entails the appropriate čəd-word following -t-əb, -du-b, -tu-b, -s-əb, or -c-əb. (See Lesson Six, especially 6.5.) Another means of conveying these concepts is by special suffixes. Contrast the following pairs of sentences:

1a. ʔuƛ'ukʷtub čəxʷ ʔu ʔə ti ʔaciɬtalbixʷ.	Did the people take you home?
1b. ʔuƛ'ukʷtubicid ʔu ti ʔaciɬtalbixʷ.	Did the people take you home?
2a. ʔuʔəƛ'tub čəd ʔə tsi luχ.	The old woman brought me.
2b. ʔuʔəƛ'tubš tsi luχ.	The old woman brought me.
3a. ʔugʷəč'təb čəɬ ʔə ti sqʷəbayʔ.	The dog looked for us.
3b. ʔugʷəč'tubuɬ ti sqʷəbayʔ.	The dog looked for us.
4a. ʔubəčdub čəd ʔə ti sqʷəbayʔ.	The dog accidentally knocked me over.
4b. ʔubəčdubš ti sqʷəbayʔ.	The dog accidentally knocked me over.

9.1a. In place of čəxʷ there is -icid, and čəd is replaced by -š. Instead of čəɬ there is -uɬ; and -uɬəd (not shown above) would substitute for čələp.

9.1b. When suffixes (rather than čəd-words) express a patient, the agent is NOT introduced by ʔə.

9.2. A čəd-word, if present, represents an agent when these patient person suffixes occur.

5. ɬuƛ'ukʷtubicid čəd.	I will take you home.
6. ɬuʔuxʷtubuɬ čələp ʔu.	Will you folks take us (somewhere)?
7. ɬuʔuxʷtubš čələp ʔu.	Will you folks take me (somewhere)?
8. ɬuƛ'ukʷtubuɬəd čəɬ.	We will take you folks home.

(The initial ɬ(u)- is an **irrealis** which here represents future time. See Lesson Thirteen.)

9.3. Person patient suffixes divide into two classes.

41

9.3a. One class goes with verbs ending in -du-b, -tu-b, -s-əb, and -c-əb.

ʔubəčdubš	…knocked me down.	ʔuʔux̌ʷtubš	…took me somewhere.
ʔubəčdubicid	…knocked you down.	ʔuʔux̌ʷtubicid	…took you somewhere.
ʔubəčdubuɫ	…knocked us down.	ʔuʔux̌ʷtubuɫ	…took us somewhere.
ʔubəčdubuɫəd	…knocked you folks down.	ʔuʔux̌ʷtubuɫəd	…took you folks somewhere.
ʔutəlawisəbš	…ran after me.	ʔuʔux̌ʷcəbš	…went [to see] me.
ʔutəlawisəbicid	…ran after you.	ʔuʔux̌ʷcəbicid	…went [to see] you.
ʔutəlawisəbuɫ	…ran after us.	ʔuʔux̌ʷcəbuɫ	…went [to see] us.
ʔutəlawisəbuɫəd	…ran after you folks.	ʔuʔux̌ʷcəbuɫəd	…went [to see] you folks.

9.3b. The other class of person patient suffixes, those belonging to the second set, follows verbs like kʷədad which end with -t-əb. Different from the first group of endings which is added to the final -(ə)b of -du-b, -tu-b, -s-əb, -c-əb, this set has dropped the -əb leaving only -t-. Where one would expect ʔukʷədatəbš, there is ʔukʷədats which becomes ʔukʷədac.[8]

(ʔukʷədats >) ʔukʷədac.	[Someone] grabbed me.
(ʔukʷədyits >) ʔukʷədyic ʔə ti ɫaʔx̌.	[Someone] took the platter from me.
(ʔukʷədatsid >) ʔukʷədacid.	[Someone] grabbed you.
ʔukʷədatubuɫ	[Someone] grabbed us.
ɫukʷədatubuɫəd	[Someone] will grab you folks.

9.4. Like čəd-words, these person patient suffixes lack forms equivalent to *him, her, it, them*.

9.5. However, there is another suffix that belongs to these person patient endings. This is the **reflexive**. Note the last sentence in each of the following sets of examples and contrast it with the others in the same set.

9a. ʔušudubš*.	[Someone] saw me.
9b. ʔušudubut čəd.	I saw myself. (Reflection)

---

[8] The s in these endings has fallen together with the preceding t becoming simply c.

10a. ʔuʔɬəd čəd.   I ate.

10b. ʔuʔɬtubš.   [Someone] fed me.

10c. ʔuʔɬtub<u>ut</u> čəd.   I fed myself.

11a. (ʔutʼucʼutsid >) ʔutʼucʼucid ʔu.   Did [someone] shoot (at) you?

11b. (ʔutʼucʼut<u>sut</u> >) ʔutʼucʼu<u>cut</u> čəxʷ ʔu.   Did you shoot yourself?

12a. (ʔuqʷuluts >) ʔuqʷuluc tsi sɬadəyʔ.   The lady hugged me.

12b. (ʔuqʷulut<u>sut</u> >) ʔuqʷulu<u>cut</u>.   He/she hugged him/herself.

From these few phrases the student can see that -ut follows -du-b, -tu-b, and presumably -s-əb and -c-əb.   (Actually, utterances with these last two endings are unrecorded.) Following the -t- of -t-əb, however, the ending is -sut which elides with the preceding -t- to give -cut. See footnote 8.

9.6. Conceptually related to the reflexive is the **reciprocal** suffix, -agʷəl. These two are contrasted in the following example sentences:

13a. ʔuʔɬt<u>ag</u>ʷ<u>əl</u> čəɬ.   We fed each other.

13b. ʔuʔɬtubut čəd.   I fed myself.

14a. ʔušud<u>ag</u>ʷ<u>əl</u> čəɬ.   We saw one another.

14b. ʔušudubut čəd.   I saw myself.

15a. ʔutʼucʼut<u>ag</u>ʷ<u>əl</u> čələp ʔu.   Did you folks shoot at one another?

15b. (ʔutʼucʼutsut >) ʔutʼucʼucut čəd.   I shot myself.

16a. ʔuqʷulut<u>ag</u>ʷ<u>əl</u>.   They hugged one another.

16b. (ʔuqʷulutsut >) ʔuqʷulucut.   He/she hugged him/herself.

17. ʔuɬəčis<u>ag</u>ʷ<u>əl</u>.   They came together., i.e., they arrived at the same place.

18. ʔubaliic<u>ag</u>ʷ<u>əl</u> čəɬ.   We forgot about each other.

9.6a. Different from the reflexive and other person patient suffixes, the reciprocal has only one form, -agʷəl, but sometimes it is pronounced as though it were spelled -əgʷəl.

9.6b. In all cases -agʷəl follows a reduced form of the preceding suffix sequence. The ending is -t-agʷəl, not -tub-agʷəl; -d-agʷəl, not -dub-agʷəl; etc. Therefore, sequences of -t(əb)-agʷəl and -t(ub)-agʷəl are both simply -t-agʷəl except that the former is very often preceded by a vowel (matching the vowel of the root) while the latter never is. In either case, the meaning is the same, so there is no ambiguity.

9.7. Dialect differences. The Southern Lushootseed equivalent of ʔušudubš, ʔušudubut, etc., is ʔulabduš, ʔulabdubut, etc.

9.8. Exercises. The student should write out one complete paradigm (list) of person patient endings including the reflexive and reciprocal for a representative verb from each class, -du-b, -tu-b, -s-əb, -c-əb, and -t(-əb). Check the lists carefully for accuracy. Then read out loud each list ten times twice a day for four days. (By following this procedure, every student will always be able to recognize the person patient suffixes.)

Gloss (translate) the following words. Several of these have stems that are new. They can be found in the glossary.

1. -ʔəɬtubicid _____   4. -dᶻəlaχadbic _____

2. -yəhubtubš _____   5. -yəcəbtubicid _____

3. -həčʔiw'dubut _____   6. -šulagʷildubut _____

LESSON TEN

ʔəs- ({as-}) stative and ʔu- ({u}) perfective prefixes; verbs expressing cognition

1a. ʔuqʼaxʷ ti stuləkʷ.	The river froze.
1b. ʔəsqʼaxʷ ti stuləkʷ.	The river is frozen.
2a. ʔuʔitut ti luX̌.	The old man fell asleep.
2b. ʔəsʔitut ti luX̌.	The old man is asleep.
3a. ʔuɬidid ti sqʷəbayʔ.	[Someone] tied the dog.
3b. ʔəsɬid ti sqʷəbayʔ.	The dog is tied.
4a. ʔuɬačʼad ti hud.	[Someone] extinguished the fire.
4b. ʔəsɬačʼ ti hud.	The fire is extinguished.

Contrast 1a with 1b and 2a with 2b. The first word in each pair of sentences is identical except for what? _____.

10.1. Up to this point every verb has begun with ʔu-.[9] The student can now see that ʔu- is a separable element called a **prefix** which contrasts with another prefix, ʔəs-.

10.2. On the basis of the English translations, one might assume that ʔu- designates past time while ʔəs- refers to the present. Such an assumption is not correct. Consider the following list of words all of which bear the prefix ʔəs-:

ʔəstagʷəxʷ*	hungry	ʔəsX̌ʼax̌*	feel cold
ʔəstaqʷuʔ	thirsty	ʔəsx̌əɬ	sick
ʔəsbəɬ	satiated, full	ʔəscʼud	sickly, run down
ʔəshiiɬ	happy	ʔəsx̌icʼil	ashamed
ʔəsqʷicʼ	indifferent, unwilling	ʔəsx̌icil	angry

_____

[9]In 9.2 there was also ɬu-. ɬu- plus ʔu- becomes simply ɬu- when speaking at a normal conversational rate. See Lesson Thirteen.

What common thread of meaning do they all share? **STOP** reading at this point to consider the answer to this question. Only after forming some sort of answer, should the student continue reading.

The above words all express conditions (or states) of mind and body.

Now add to this list the words having the ʔəs- prefix from the sentences at the beginning of this lesson numbered 1b through 4b writing them in the blanks on the left.

_____	_____
_____	_____
_____	_____
_____	_____
_____	_____

In the blanks on the right write the English glosses appropriate for the Lushootseed words on the left. Omit *is* from the glosses. (It is required by the grammar of the English sentences that translate the Lushootseed sentences, but it is not part of the Lushootseed verb's meaning.)

10.3. From this additional list the student can see that it is not just conditions of the mind and body that ʔəs- refers to but rather to states in general. Therefore, ʔəs- is called the **stative prefix.** It can be used in the present, past or future because its meaning makes no reference to time at all. Whether one says *is frozen, was frozen,* or *will be frozen*, the <u>state</u> of being frozen is unchanged.

10.4. The stative prefix is not used with words that are inherently or intrinsically stative such as haac *long/tall (thing)*, hikʷ *big*, haʔɬ *good*, luχ *old*, and x̌ikʷ *ugly*.[10] In other

---

[10]With appropriate suffixation, however, these words are changed into verbs that do take prefixes. Here are several examples.

ʔəsx̌ik'ʷəb čəd.	I'm lonesome.
ʔux̌ik'ʷəb čəxʷ ʔu.	Did you get lonesome?
ʔəsluλ'əb ti sqʷəbayʔ.	The dog is old.
ʔuhaʔɬil.	[The weather] became good.
ʔuhigʷild.	[Someone] made [something] bigger.

(Often a final kʷ- sound becomes gʷ when a vowel follows as in this last example.)

words, ʔəs- makes stative verbs out of roots that are not already stative in their core meaning.

10.5. The prefix ʔu-, on the other hand, indicates verbs that express events, actions, processes, and the like. It is called the **perfective prefix.** (The meaning of this name is explained in the next lesson.)

10.6. Some very common verbs expressing cognition and perception typically bear the -dxʷ/-dub suffixes (See 5.3.) and the stative prefix. The three most frequently occurring are presented in the short sentences below.

> 5. ʔəslax̌dub čəɬ ʔə ti sqʷəbayʔ.   The dog remembers us.
>
> 6. ʔə(s)šudub ʔə ti čačas ti sqʷəbayʔ.   The boy sees the dog.
>
> 7. ʔəs(h)aydxʷ[11] čəxʷ ʔu tsi lux̌.   Do you know the old woman?

10.7. Dialect differences.

10.7.a The Northern Lushootseed ʔəstagʷəxʷ *hungry* is matched by ʔəscəwəɬ in Southern Lushootseed.

10.7b. There is no exact equivalent to x̌ʷax̌ in Southern Lushootseed where x̌ʷuxʷi(l) is used. Thus, Southern x̌ʷuxʷi(l) corresponds to both the Northern x̌ʷuxʷil *cold state of objects* and x̌ʷax̌ *person feels cold.*

10.8. Vocabulary comment. Whereas English uses the three words *burn, fire,* and *firewood,* Lushootseed has the one word, hud. Sometimes hud is also used to designate wood in general. The reader (or listener) depends on context to distinguish these different meanings of hud.

The range of meaning that many Lushootseed roots have usually does not match closely the semantic range of the nearest English equivalent. Often, in fact, the concepts that Lushootseed speakers subsume under a particular word surprise those who speak English. A case in point is x̌ikʷ. Ponder the following:

---

[11]Letters in parentheses represent sounds that are not pronounced in a particular circumstance. In this case the h-sound is lost following an s-sound. If the prefix were ʔu-, the h̲ would be pronounced.

x̌ikʷ	ugly (in appearance or personality), mean, rude, inclined to 'rough' talk; strange in appearance.
ʔəsx̌ikʷʔil	in a mean mood.
x̌ikʷəb	be still (imperative), be quiet.
ʔəsx̌ikʷʔəb	lonesome.

10.9. Exercises and Homework. Translate the following into Lushootseed:

1. The dog is thirsty. _____.

2. Are you hungry? _____.

3. Is the old man lonesome? _____.

4. The old woman put the fire out. _____.

5. Did the boy tie the dog up? _____.

6. Is the river frozen? _____.

7. I remember it. _____.

8. Are we happy? _____.

9. Do you know the girl? _____.

10. [Someone] took the dog home. _____.

11. Did the girl take the mat? _____.

12. I don't feel like it. (Said in response to a request or suggestion to do something.)

_____.

LESSON ELEVEN
Tense and aspect

(In places this lesson involves fairly abstract discussions. Students are not expected to grasp all of it immediately. Much of what is described here will be understood only gradually as more and more texts are read. Students should not, therefore, be discouraged if there is much they do not fully comprehend at first. Rather, they should take pleasure in probing a different culture's system of organizing the realm of time.)

11.1. **Tense,** that is to say, <u>present</u>, <u>past</u>, and <u>future</u>, is forced upon speakers of English by the grammar. Every sentence must be expressed in one of these three categories because tense in English is obligatory. With every sentence English speakers must locate the event before, after, or during the moment of speaking (or with reference to some other event).

11.2. In Lushootseed, on the other hand, tense is not obligatory; usually it is not mentioned. Instead, Lushootseed grammar is much concerned with **aspect** which describes the period of time within which an event or process occurs.

11.2a. English also marks aspect. Differences like *is going* versus *goes* and *has gone* versus *went* are aspectual and obligatory. But many aspectual differences are optional in English. Some of these are formed with phrases like *burst into tears, cry by fits and starts*, and *do over and over*.

In some cases the difference in meaning between two English verb roots is primarily aspectual. Consider *beat* versus *hit*. The first is <u>repetitive</u> while the second is <u>momentaneous</u>.

11.2b. All these sorts of differences are aspectual. They concern the *temporal how of an event, the lapse of time in which the act is done -- not when it is done (which is tense).*

11.3. Lushootseed verbs are either static or dynamic. If static, they typically bear the stative prefix ʔəs- presented in Lesson Ten. If dynamic, they divide into two groups called **perfective** and **imperfective**.

49

11.3a. Perfective verbs are normally designated by the prefix ʔu-; however, speakers not infrequently omit this prefix when context clearly establishes this aspect as the only possibility.

With the perfective aspect, an act is viewed as *a single whole* without concern for the various phases involved in the event. The speaker looks upon the action in its *entirety* when ʔu- is used.

11.3b. In contrast to the perfective, imperfective verbs distinguish various phases of an activity. In most dialects of Lushootseed there are two contrasting imperfective prefixes, the **progressive** lə- and the **progressive state** ləs-. However, the Swinomish, Skagit, Sauk-Suiattle, and some Snohomish speakers have a third imperfect prefix, the **continuous**, ləcu-.

11.3c. These five prefixes form a mutually exclusive set occurring immediately before the verb stem:

$$
\text{(other possible prefixes)} \quad
\begin{array}{l}
\text{ʔəs-} \\
\text{ʔu-} \\
\text{lə-} \\
\text{ləs-} \\
\text{ləcu-}
\end{array}
\quad \text{verb stem}
$$

11.4. The sentences below illustrate a common use of the progressive prefix.

1. ləʔuxʷ ti čʼačʼas.   The boy is/was/will be going.

2. ləʔuxʷtxʷ ti čʼačʼas.   [Someone] is/was/will be taking the boy somewhere.

3. lətʼukʷʷ čəxʷ ʔu.   Are/were you on your way home?
                                             (or)
                               Will you be on your way home?

4. ləʔəƛʼ čəd.   I am/was/will be coming.

5. ləʔibəš ti luƛ.   The old man is/was/will be walking.

6. lətəlawil ti čʼačʼas.   The boy is/was/will be running.

11.4a. Contrast the six sentences above with those presented in Lessons One and Two, all of which begin with the prefix ʔu-. The difference is not one of tense because all example sentences with ʔu- could as well be rendered in English with the present or even occasionally the future. Instead the difference is aspectual.

11.4b. With lə- the speaker views the action as ongoing and continuous. It often occurs with verb stems that refer to movement through space as in the sentences above.

11.4c. The progressive prefix is also heard frequently with stems that incorporate the idea of becoming or developing. Typically, these stems end in -il. With such stems lə- designates movement through time.

7. ləlux̌il čəxʷ.	As you grow up ...
8. ləɬax̌il.	[It] is/was/will be becoming night.
9. ləxʷakʷʷil čəd.	I am/was/will be getting tired.
10. ləqʷiqʷʷil*.	[He] is/was/will be getting stronger.

11.4d. Comparing sentences 1 - 6 with 7 - 10 shows that both time and distance are conceptualized the same way with lə-.

11.5. When an activity which ordinarily takes place in one location is performed while moving from one place to another, lə- is again the appropriate prefix.

11a. ləťilib tsi k̓aʔk̓aʔ.	Crow is/was singing as she travels/traveled along.
11b. ʔuťilib tsi k̓aʔk̓aʔ.	Crow sings/sang.
12a. ləťixʷicut ti sqʷəbayʔ.	The dog is shaking himself off as he goes along.
12b. ʔuťixʷicut ti sqʷəbayʔ.	The dog shakes/shook himself off.
13a. ləʔəy'dxʷ ti ʔaciɬtalbixʷ.	As he travels/traveled, he finds/found people.
13b. ʔuʔəy'dxʷ[12] ti ʔaciɬtalbixʷ.	He finds/found people.

Occasionally, however, a temporal rather than spacial notion dominates in these stems designating activities normally done in one place. In such cases lə- adds a **graduative** notion, e.g.,

ləx̌ucusitəb ti ɬukʷaɬ.   *The sun's face is gradually wrapped up.*[13]

---

[12]See footnote 4 of 5.3.

[13]Rather than *setting*, the sun in Lushootseed cosmology is wrapped up or squeezed into a bag at dusk.

11.6. Optional: A related concept conveyed by lə- refers to activities done serially, one subsequent to another. Here are two examples from a text talking about Bobcat and his hunting:

bələ̲t'uc'ud ti dəč'uʔ.	Again he shot one.
gʷəl bələ̲xʷit'il.	And it fell [out of a tree].
bələ̲t'uc'ud.	He shot another.
bələ̲t'uc'ud ti ʔiɬlaq.	He shot the last one too.
həd ʔiw'təb ʔə ti stubš.	The man put [them] in the house.
gʷəl lə̲k'iɬid ti q̓čic*, ti ʔiɬičəd.	and hung on a peg [first] the bow, [then] the quiver.

11.7. The aspect prefix ləs-, **progressive state.**

11.7a. This prefix designates a state viewed as contingent upon or intimately involved with some dynamic event. (The following illustrative sentences are grammatically more complex than students can fully understand at this point. A general feel for the situation that prompts the use of ləs- is all they need be concerned with here.)

14. ləskʷaxʷad   čəd   dxʷʔal   sxʷiʔs   kʷi   gʷəsbakʷɫs.
     helping-him   I   so-that   not   get-hurt-he
     I am helping him so that he won't get hurt.

15. ləsx̌əɬx̌əɬačiʔ čəd   yəx̌i   čəd   tuləd̓əq'il.
     hurting-hands I   because   I   crawled
     My hands are hurting because I crawled.

11.7b. It is required when a state is maintained while progressing through space.

16a. ləsʔitut ti č'ač'as.	The sleeping boy (is being carried somewhere).
16b. ʔəsʔitut ti č'ač'as.	The boy is asleep.
17a. ləsʔibəš čəɬ.	We are walking together.
17b. ləʔibəš čəɬ.	We are walking.
18a. ləskʷədad ti q̓čic*.	He is carrying the bow.
18b. ʔəskʷədad ti q̓čic.	He is holding the bow.
19. ləscil ti jəsəds* ʔal ti səʔibəšs.	Her feet are protected while she walks.

11.8. The fifth aspect prefix is ləcu-, **continuous.** Consider the following sentences:

20. ləcuyayus tsi x̌ax̌acʼapəd*.	Ant is working.
21. ləcutʼilib tsi kʼaʔkʼaʔ.	Crow is singing.
22. ləcupʼayəq ʔə ti sdəxʷił.	[He] is hewing out a hunting canoe.
23. ləcutʼixʷicut ti sqʷəbayʔ.	The dog is shaking himself off.
24. ləcuqəlb.	[It] is raining.
25. ləcuqʷat ʔu.	Is [it] snowing?

11.8a. Typically, lə- involves movement from one location to another while ləcu- is used with activities that are ordinarily in one place or events that happen in one place.

11.8b. However, occasionally speakers do use ləcu- with verbs that designate movement through space. With these ləcu- adds the notion of *habitual* or *regular* performance. Compare these two pairs of sentences:

26a. ləcutəlawil čəd.	I am running (as part of my daily exercise program).
26b. lətəlawil čəd.	I am running (at this moment).
27a. ləcuʔibibəš ti sčətxʷəd.	Bear would be walking about aimlessly.
27b. ləʔibəš ti sčətxʷəd.	Bear is/was walking (at the moment).

11.8c. Conversely, there are a few patient oriented verb stems whose root meaning includes movement through space that do not permit lə- (except in its serial use (11.6)). These are verbs of the class taking -d, -t-əb immediately following the root (6.1, 9.3b). Verbs of this type use ləcu- instead of -- and with the same meaning as -- lə- in 11.4. Such a verb is čalad *chase [someone]*. Consider the following briefly described event:

ʔuluudəxʷ[14] ti stab.	[He] heard something.
ʔudᶻalq ʷusəxʷ.	[He] looked over his shoulder.
ʔušudxʷəxʷ ti hikʷ sx̌alqəb.	[He] saw a big monster.
ləcučalad.	[It] was chasing [him].

11.8d. Many Lushootseed speakers do not use ləcu-. It is not heard in Southern Lushootseed at all and many Snohomish do not use it. However, it is very much a part

---

[14]The significance of -əxʷ is explained in 14.2 - 14.3c.

of the aspect system for the Sauk-Suiattle, the Swinomish and all those along the Skagit River.

For people who do not have ləcu- in their speech, other verbal strategies are available to render nearly the same concept. These include (1) the use of adverbs (Lesson Seventeen) such as ckʷaqid *always*, (2) combinations of prefixes such as χu- (Lesson Thirteen) plus lə-, (3) the repetition of a verb several times (each one bearing the prefix ʔu-) or (4) **reduplications** (repetitions of part or all of the root), and (5) using lə- in situations where the Skagit (and some Snohomish speakers) would say ləcu-.

11.9. Of the five aspectual prefixes presented in lessons Ten and Eleven, two are often omitted. When context makes clear that the verb requires ʔu- or lə-, these two are not said. The omission of ʔu- is particularly frequent. (In the texts ʔu- has sometimes been replaced, but all such additions are in editorial brackets, [ ].)

11.10. Commands are primarily signalled by vocal intonation. They are further characterized by the absence of all prefixes.[15] Commands issued to more than one person often include the particle ɫi which follows the verb occurring where čələp would otherwise be.

11.11. Dialect differences.

11.11a. The following brief list sets out those lexical differences between Southern and Northern Lushootseed which occur for the first time in this lesson.

Southern	Northern	
wələx̌ʷ	qʷiqʷʷil	strong (muscular)
c̓acus	q̓čic	bow (archery)
bəčlulaʔ	λ̓aλ̓ac̓apəd	ant
ǰəšəd	ǰəsəd	foot / lower leg

(With this last pair compare č̓ač̓aš instead of č̓ač̓as, and čaləš instead of čaləs (1.4, 4.7c). In the three cases š corresponds to s. Many words exhibit this correspondence between Southern and Northern Lushootseed.)

---

[15]To this statement one must except word building (that is, **derivational**) prefixes.

11.11b. In place of xʷakʷˀil some Upriver Skagit use q̓ʷəɬəb. For others, the latter word is an intensified counterpart of the former -- something like *exhausted* compared to *tired*.

11.12. Vocabulary comment. The Northern Lushootseed word for *bow (archery)* is derived from q̓əč-, q̓č- *bend, bent, crooked* and (possibly) the suffix -ič which by **dissimilation** becomes -ic.

The Northern Lushootseed word for *ant* is built upon ƛ̓acˀ meaning *cinch, cinch up, tighten*. The ending -apəd refers to the *waist* or to a *belt* and the doubled first part (a process called reduplication (11.8d)) means *small*. Thus, ƛ̓aƛ̓acˀapəd is the *Little Cinched Up (One)*.

11.13. Exercises.

I. On file cards write the three aspectual prefixes lə-, ləs- and ləcu- (one per card) in the upper left hand corner. Add the grammatical name of the prefix in the upper right hand corner. Below copy from the lesson each explanation of use or meaning provided for the prefix.

II. On a separate sheet of paper, write out answers to the following questions without consulting the cards just prepared or the lesson. When finished, reread the lesson to check the answers.

(1) Typically, ləcu- occurs with verbs having what kind of meaning?

(2) What is the difference in meaning between ʔəs- and ləs-?

(3) How does ʔu- differ from ləcu-?

(4) Why does čalad *chase [someone]* take ləcu- instead of lə-?

III. Gloss each of the following words:

ʔukʷədad _____ .

ʔəskʷədad _____ .

ləskʷədad _____ .

ʔut̕ilib _____ .

lət̕ilib _____ .

ləcut̕ilib _____ .

ʔutəlawil _____ .

lətəlawil _____ .

ləcutəlawil _____ .

LESSON TWELVE

The s- prefix; have and have not; d- paradigm affixes

Leaf through the previous lessons to find all the Lushootseed nouns presented thus far. Write them in two columns on a separate sheet of paper. On the left put those nouns that begin with s̱; on the right fill in all the nouns that do not begin with s̱. Following those words that are restricted to only a part of the Lushootseed territory, add in parentheses abbreviations representing the regions where they do occur, e.g., čačaš (SL), spaʔc (Swin.), etc.

12.1. A third of the nouns presented in the first eleven lessons begin with s̱. Except for sup'qs *hair seal* all these nouns with initial s̱ have another consonant as the second sound. In each case the s̱ of the **consonant cluster** is actually a prefix. Because nouns with this prefix s- are so numerous, Lushootseed glossaries and dictionaries list them under the second consonant rather than by the initial s-. Thus, sčətxʷəd *black bear* is found under č̱, not under s̱.

On the other hand, if a vowel follows an initial s̱, that s̱ is not a prefix. Therefore, sup'qs is listed under s̱. (Remember, ʔ is a consonant. Find sʔuladxʷ in the glossary.)

The same practice is used with verbs. They are listed by the letter for the first sound of the stem -- **not** the prefix.

Study the following sentences:

1a. ʔah ʔu kʷi gʷəqʷuʔs.	Does he/she have [any] water?
1b. xʷiʔ.	No.
1c. xʷiʔ kʷi gʷəqʷuʔs.	He/she does not have [any] water.
2a. ʔah ʔu kʷi gʷəhuds.	Does he/she have [any] wood?
2b. xʷiʔ.	No.
2c. xʷiʔ kʷi gʷəhuds.	He/she does not have [any] wood.
3a. ʔah ʔu kʷi gʷəsqʷəbayʔs.	Does he/she have a dog?
3b. xʷiʔ.	No.
3c. xʷiʔ kʷi gʷəsqʷəbayʔs.	He/she does not have a dog.
4a. ʔah ʔu kʷi gʷəsʔuladxʷs.	Does he/she have [any] salmon?
4b. ʔah ti sʔuladxʷs.	He/she has [some] salmon.

57

5a. ʔah ʔu kʷi gʷəsčəbids.[16]   Does he/she have [any] fir bark?

5b. ʔah ti sčəbids.   He/she has [some] fir bark.

12.2. Affirmative answers to questions in Lushootseed typically do not include ʔi, the word meaning *yes*. Instead, speakers simply make a short affirmative statment as in 4b and 5b. Where English style would expect something like, *Yes, he/she has some salmon*, Lushootseed style omits the *yes*.

12.3. The above example sentences depart rather far in formation from their English equivalents. For example, a literal translation of sentence 1a would be, *Is there his/her water?* And 1c would be, *[There] is not his/her water.*

12.3a. When something is remote, hypothetical, or simply nonexistent, its noun is preceded by kʷi instead of ti.

12.3b. The prefix gʷ- is called **subjunctive**. (When it precedes a consonant as in the above example sentences, it is written as gʷə-. Before vowels it is simply gʷ-.) This subjunctive prefix is used when questioning, denying, or doubting. With nouns, speakers often omit it because kʷi expresses much the same idea. With verbs, some speakers usually omit kʷi, others tend to omit gʷ-. (In completing the exercises to this and subsequent lessons, however, the student should not omit either kʷi or gʷ-.)

12.3c. The suffix -s represents someone or something in relation to someone or something else.[17] As will be seen below, this suffix also relates someone to actions and states. Because of this last fact, it is best for the student not to think of -s as corresponding very

---

[16]Fir bark was a very important source of fuel for the Lushootseed in former times.

[17]In traditional grammar this suffix and its equivalents in other languages is called **possessive**. This term is a poor one however. In what sense does someone possess *his father*? And if one could make a case for claiming that she possesses *her hand*, it must, at least, be admitted that this possession is very different from that of *her book*. Also consider the ambiguities of the phrase *his picture*. Is it one he purchased; did he paint it; or is it a picture of him? Because the term *possessive* is often inappropriate and always imprecise, this description of Lushootseed does not use it.

closely in meaning to *his, her, its* even though these English words are often used in translating sentences with -s.

12.3d. When the speaker chooses to be explicit about the person (or item) involved in the relationship, specific mention is made of that person by means of ʔə. Compare the following:

x̌ʷubts	his paddle	x̌ʷubt ʔə ti hədli	Henry's paddle
sqʷəbayʔs	her dog	sqʷəbayʔ ʔə tsi mali	Mary's dog
šaw̓s	its bone	šaw̓ ʔə ti sqʷəbayʔ	the dog's bone

As can be seen, the -s suffix is replaced by ʔə plus a noun denoting the other member of the relationship.

12.3e. People's names require ti or tsi (or kʷi, kʷsi) just like other nouns.

Translate the sentences below into Lushootseed:

We looked for Mary's dog. _____ .

It ate the old woman's salmon. _____ .

She roasted the boy's salmon. _____ .

He took the old man's paddle. _____ .

12.4. Compare the following words with one another and with those listed in 12.3d above. Provide the missing English gloss on each blank.

dx̌ʷubt	my paddle	x̌ʷubt čəł	_____
dsqʷəbayʔ	_____	sqʷəbayʔ čəł	our dog
dšaw̓	my bone	šaw̓ čəł	our bone
adx̌ʷubt	your paddle	x̌ʷubtləp	(the) paddle of you folks
adsqʷəbayʔ	your dog	sqʷəbayʔləp	_____
adšaw̓	_____	šaw̓ləp	(the) bone of you folks

12.4a. These three affixes plus čəł along with the -s suffix of 12.3 - 12.3d form a rather peculiar set. Two members are prefixes, d- and ad-; two are suffixes, -ləp and -s; and one is an interloper from the čəd-word paradigm, namely čəł.

12.4b. Person markers of this **paradigm** (list of items belonging to the same class) are also different in that there is a form for *he/his, she/her(s),* and *it/its* which the čəd-words and person patient suffixes lack. (See 12.5 below.)

12.4c. In the following sentences discover the relative order of the three prefixes ad-, gʷ-, and s-.

6a. ʔah ʔu kʷi gʷadsqʷəbayʔ.	Do you have a dog?
6b. ʔah ti dsqʷəbayʔ.	I have a dog.
7a. ʔah ʔu kʷi gʷadsčəbid.	Do you have [any] fir bark?
7b. ʔah ti dsčəbid.	I have [some] fir bark.

12.4d. In later sentences it will be seen that d-, like ad-, also occurs between gʷ(ə)- and s-. This arrangement is summarized below:

$$g^w\text{-}\quad d\text{-}\quad (s\text{-})$$
$$ad\text{-}$$

12.4e. Although čəł has been brought into this paradigm it is not well integrated. Except for čəł members of this paradigm are all affixes and can co-occur with čəd-words as is shown here:

adstaləł čəd.	I am your nephew/niece.
dstaləł čəxʷ.	You are my nephew/niece.
staləłs čəd.	I am his/her nephew/niece.
staləłs čəxʷ.	You are his/her nephew/niece.
staləłləp čəd.	I am the nephew/niece of you folks.
staləł čəł čəxʷ.	NOT ACCEPTABLE. (See Lesson Nineteen.)

Even though čəł is used to mean *our*, etc., it cannot occur in the same formations with čəd-words.   However, when čəł is serving in its original function as a čəd-word, occurrence with this d-paradigm is grammatical:

adstətaləł čəł.	We are your nephews/nieces.
stətaləłs čəł.	We are his/her nephews/nieces.
	(stətaləł is the plural of staləł.)

12.5. The three person paradigms presented thus far are brought together here.

First person	Singular	čəd	-š/-c	d-
	Plural	čəɬ	-(ub)uɬ	(čəɬ)
Second person	Singular	čəxʷ	-(i)cid	ad-
	Plural	čələp	-(ub)uɬəd	-ləp
Third person				-s

In traditional terminology forms equivalent to *I, me, my, mine,* and *we, us, our(s)* are called **first person**; *you, your(s)* **second person**; and *he, him, his, she, her(s), it, its* and *they, them, their(s)* **third person**. These terms are used in this reader from here on.

12.6. There is a means of distinguishing plural from singular in the third person (although speakers of Lushootseed feel relatively little need to use it). Compare the following sentences:

8a. ʔuʔəy'dxʷ čəd ti sqʷəbayʔs.   I found his/her dog.

8b. ʔuʔəy'dxʷ čəd ti sqʷəbayʔs əlgʷəʔ.   I found their dog.

9a. ʔəstagʷəxʷ ʔu.   Is he/she hungry?

9b. ʔəstagʷəxʷ ʔu həlgʷəʔ.   Are they hungry?

When əlgʷəʔ follows a vowel, it acquires an <u>h</u> to facilitate pronunciation as in 9b above.

12.7. Exercises. Translate the following sentences into Lushootseed:

1. Do they have a hunting canoe? _____.

2. Do you have any crab? _____.

3. We have [some] fir bark. _____.

4. Do you folks have [any] water? _____.

5. Do you have a mat? _____.

6. I have [some] wood. _____.

7. We have [some] salmon. _____.

8. They have [some] arrow(s). _____.

LESSON THIRTEEN
General prefixes

13.1. Five Lushootseed prefixes can be added not only to verbs but to most other word types as well including nouns, prepositions, and any other class of word so long as it functions as the main word in a predicate or complement. (The terms *predicate* and *complement* are defined in Lesson Sixteen.) Predicate adverbs (17.2) can also bear these prefixes. These five, because of their wide distribution, are called **general prefixes**.

gʷ-	**subjunctive** (12.3b, 13.4, 14.4b)
ƛ̕u-	**habitual** (13.2)
ɫu-	**irrealis** (9.2, 13.3, 13.4)
tu-	**past** (13.5)
bə-	**additive** (13.6)

13.2. ƛ̕u- marks an act or state as being habitual. It is usually rendered in English with the words *used to* or *would* if the time is past, or by *generally* or *usually* when discussing events and states not bound by temporal considerations. For the future, however, there is often no concise way of expressing ƛ̕u- in English.

1. ƛ̕uxʷakʷ'ʷil čəd ʔəbil'əs čəd[18] ʔəstagʷʷəxʷ.   I <u>generally</u> get tired if I am hungry.

2. ƛ̕uləx̌ilič əlgʷəʔ.   It <u>would</u> get light over them.

3. ƛ̕ulət̕əd ti ƛ̕uƛ̕isəd ʔə ti šəbad.   He <u>would</u> flip the <u>habitual</u> arrows of the enemy away.

13.3. ɫu- shows that an event or state is expected in the future or, at least, that it might occur. At the moment of speaking, however, the event or state has not become a reality. A few examples are given in 9.2. Several others follow here.

4. ɫugəlk̕ čəd.   I <u>might</u> get tangled.

5. lilcut! ɫubaʔkʷɫ čəxʷ.   Get away! You <u>might/will</u> get hurt.

---

[18]This position of čəd ahead of its verb is discussed in Lesson Seventeen.

6. ʔal kʷi ɬudukʷəɬdat   tomorrow

7. ɬubəščəb čəxʷ.   You <u>will</u> be a mink.

13.4. The irrealis, ɬu-, and subjunctive, gʷ-, have a somewhat similar meaning from the English speaker's perspective. On occasion they are both glossed as *might*. However, gʷ- marks a situation as doubtful (when not simply contrary to fact) whereas ɬu- imparts the idea of expectation.

13.5. tu- designates past, often remote, time.

8. ʔuʔatabəd ti <u>tus</u>čʼistxʷs.   Her <u>former</u> husband died.

9. <u>tu</u>qʼiyaƛ̓əd ti <u>tus</u>čʼistxʷs. Slug <u>had been</u> her <u>former</u> husband.

10. <u>tu</u>huyucut əlgʷəʔ.   They prepar<u>ed</u> themselves.

11. <u>tu</u>čʼagʷacut.   [They] bath<u>ed</u>.

12. <u>tu</u>xʷəcdaliɬəd.   [They] fast<u>ed</u>.

13. ʔal ti <u>tu</u>dukʷəɬdat   yesterday

14. <u>tu</u>ʔal ləliʔ swatixʷtəd.   He <u>was</u> in another country.

13.6. bə- marks an act or state as occurring *again, anew, once more,* or a noun as being *additional, another.* It is called the additive prefix.

15. <u>bə</u>ʔibəš ti bəščəb.   Mink walked <u>some</u> <u>more</u>.

16. <u>bə</u>ʔəy'dxʷ ti sʔuladxʷ.   <u>Again</u> he found a salmon.

17. ɬax̌il gʷəl <u>bə</u>ləx̌il.   It's night and [then] <u>again</u> it's day.

18. s(h)adᶻəb čəd čəda[19] <u>bə</u>stibtib. I'm tall and I'm strong <u>too</u>.

19. cqʷib tsi <u>bə</u>pʼuay̓.   <u>Also</u> Flounder got in on it.

13.7. The habitual, past and irrealis comprise a subset of general prefixes based on their similar form, a single consonant plus the u-vowel. Each of them has three different pronunciations depending on what follows.

---

[19]čəda *and I* is derived from čəd *I* plus the element -a *and.* s(h)adᶻəb čəd + bəstibtib čəd *I am tall.* + *I am strong too.* becomes s(h)adᶻəb čəd <u>čəda</u> bəstibtib. See 21.7.

	1	2	3
	ƛ̕u-	ƛ̕(u)-	ƛ̕ə-
	tu-	t(u)-	tə-
	ɬu-	ɬ(u)-	ɬə-

13.7a. Immediately before a stem (as in all examples above) these three prefixes are pronounced as spelled in list 1.

13.7b. Immediately before a vowel, however, these prefixes lose their own vowel. To indicate this loss, the u-vowel is written in parentheses as in list 2. (Whatever is written in parentheses in Lushootseed orthography is not pronounced but understood to be present **etymologically**.)

13.7c. When a prefix consisting of only a single consonant separates ƛ̕u-, etc., from the stem, then these prefixes retain their full u-vowel as in list 1.

13.7d. When one or more prefixes of the form consonant + vowel or consonant + vowel + consonant separates ƛ̕u-, tu-, or ɬu- from the stem, then these latter prefixes are pronounced as in list 3. However, in spelling the u-vowel is retained.

13.8. Except for ɬu- and tu- which are mutually exclusive, general prefixes can co-occur.

13.8a. The position of general prefixes, except for bə-, is fixed relative to one another.

$$g^w\text{-} \quad ƛ̕u\text{-} \quad \begin{matrix} tu\text{-} \\ \\ ɬu\text{-} \end{matrix} \quad (+ \text{ other possible prefixes}) \quad stem$$

13.8b. The position of bə- relative to the other general prefixes is meaningful. It is usually just to the right of tu-/ɬu-, but not always. Meaning influences its location. For example, ƛ̕u-bə-ɬax̌ focuses attention on it *being night again* when something would happen, while bə-ƛ̕u-ɬax̌ is the *reoccurence* of something that *would happen at night*.

13.9. Dialect differences. The Northern Lushootseed word for mink, bəščəb, is matched by c̓əbal̕qid in Southern Lushootseed.

13.10. Vocabulary comment. Compare the Lushootseed ways of saying *yesterday* and *tomorrow*:

ʔal ti tudukʷəɬdat   *yesterday*

ʔal kʷi ɬudukʷəɬdat   *tomorrow*

The stem dukʷəɬdat means literally *change day*. What has changed is *yesterday*. What will change is *tomorrow*.

13.11. Exercises. The following excerpts from various Lushootseed texts involve vocabulary and some grammar that has not yet been presented. Each line, however, has an English translation. The student is to read through each of these looking for all cases of general prefixes. Each one is to be circled along with its English gloss whether that be a whole word or a part of a word. Be alert to the alternation that some prefixes undergo. (The first has been done as an example.)

One

1. tuʔuluɬəxʷ ti bəščəb ʔi ti qawʼqs.   Mink and Raven started out by canoe.

2. tugʷəčʼədaxʷ əlgʷəʔ kʷi sləxil.   They looked for the daylight.

3. tuləčʼitil əlgʷəʔ.   They drew near.

4. ƛuləxiləxʷ əlgʷəʔ.   It would get light over them.

5. ƛubələbəsad.   It would again get dark.

6. tuɬəgʷɬ əlgʷəʔ ti qʼilʼbids.   They left their canoe.

7. tugʷaxʷ.   [They] walked.

8. tugʷaxʷəxʷ əlgʷəʔ.   They walked now.

9. tuɬčil dxʷʔal ti ʔaciɬtalbixʷ.   [They] arrived to the people.

Two

10. ɬubəščəbəxʷ čəxʷ.   You will be a mink [from] now [on].

11. ɬupʼaƛaƛ ɬuʔal tudiʔ čaʔkʷ.   [You] will be a no-account there by the water.

12. ɬulədzəkʷdzəkʷ čəxʷ ʔal ti qəlʼqəladiʔ.   You will wander about in the snags [of driftwood].

13. tuhuyiləxʷ bəščəb.   He became a mink.

14. tuhuyil pʼaƛaƛ.   He became a no-account.

15. ʔah ti bəščəb.   There is Mink.

16. ləd^zək ᵂd^zək ᵂ uʔx ᵂ ʔal ti   He is still wandering about in the
    qəl'qəladiʔ ʔal ti čaʔk ᵂ.   snags [of driftwood] at the shore.

Three

17. bəq ᵂuʔq ᵂaʔ ʔal ti čad.   He drank again [and again every]where.

18. bəɬčiləx ᵂ.   He arrived again.

19. bəʔəy'dx ᵂəx ᵂ ti sʔuladx ᵂ.   Again he found salmon.

20. bək ᵂədalik ᵂəx ᵂ ʔə ti sʔuladx ᵂ. He caught more salmon.

Four

21. ƛuƛ'uc'utəb ti qc'ap.   Kitsap would be shot at.

22. x̌ ᵂul' ƛuɬəƛ'əd ti ƛuƛ'isəd ʔə ti   [But] he would just flip away the
    šəbad.   enemy's habitual arrows.

23. x ᵂiʔ k ᵂi g ᵂəƛ'usƛals ʔal ti   They could not enter his flesh.
    c'uk ᵂəbs.

24. day ti sq'əd^zuʔs ti ƛudəx ᵂƛ'al   It is only his hair where the arrows
    ʔə ti ƛ'isəd.   would enter.

25. ƛutux̌ ᵂ ƛubəʔabyitəb.   He would simply be given more [arrows by
                                       the enemy].

26. ɬubək ᵂədadəx ᵂ.   He will grab another [enemy arrow from out
                                       of his hair].

27. g ᵂəl ɬubəƛ'uc'ud.   And he will shoot [it] back at [them].

SUMMARY LIST OF INFLECTIONAL AFFIXES

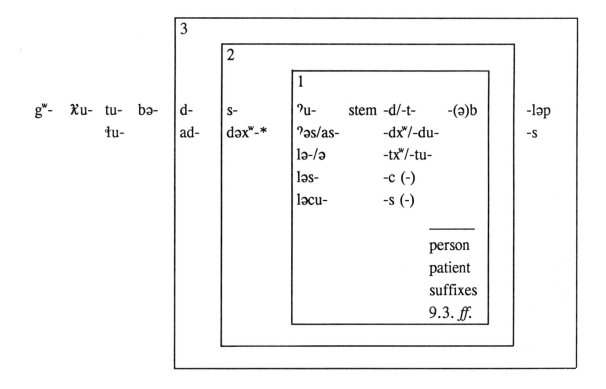

All inflection within the rectangle labeled 1 is exclusively verbal. That encompassed by rectangle 2 marks the main word in subordinate clauses (Lesson Twenty-one) and also a large class of nouns. Inflection within rectangle 3 is the person system appropriate for structures in rectangle 2. (The prefix dəxʷ- is replaced by səxʷ- in Southern Lushootseed.)

LESSON FOURTEEN
Clitics

14.1. Most inflectional affixes have now been presented. There remain to present, however, several **clitics.** These are the topic of the this lesson.

14.1a. Clitics might be thought of as 'semi-suffixes'. They are pronounced as though they were the last part of the word they follow -- the way *n't* fits together with *do* in English *don't*. Grammatically, however, clitics are separable words. They occur in various places within the sentence attaching to several different word types.

14.1b. Furthermore, the phonological (i.e., pronunciation) unit clitics form with the word to which they attach is less 'cohesive' than that which binds suffix to stem. Consider the suffix -d/-t-. When this suffix ends a word, speakers use -d; but when other suffixes follow, they say -t-. Compare k̉ʷədad *grabs someone/something* to k̉ʷədatubuɫ *grabs us* (instead of *k̉ʷədadubuɫ). When a clitic is added, however, the 'final -d' remains, e.g., k̉ʷədadəxʷ *grabs someone/something now* (rather than *k̉ʷədatəxʷ). (The ending əxʷ represents the clitic axʷ *now* as explained in 14.2a below. See also 14.3.)

14.2. There are two sets of clitics in Lushootseed. One of these has just one member, axʷ *now.* The other is a class of five person markers closely related to the čəd-words.

14.2a. All six clitics begin with a vowel which is a when stressed, ə otherwise. Clitics are stressed when the word to which they attach has no vowels (apart from those in prefixes) or no vowels other than ə.

14.2b. If a clitic attaches to a word ending in a vowel, an epenthetic h keeps the two vowels distinct, e.g., čubəhəxʷ from čubə *go up from shore* plus axʷ *now.*

14.3. The most frequently heard clitic in Lushootseed is axʷ conveniently, although somewhat misleadingly, glossed as *now.* More precisely, axʷ means that the situation is now different from what it had been, that a new act or condition is now in effect. The following two sets of sentences illustrate this concept:

huy, q⁴ax̌ʷ ti bəščəb.   Then Mink woke up.

gʷəl (h)uy, haydx̌ʷəx̌ʷ.   And then he knew [what had happened].

huy, bək̓ʷədalikʷəx̌ʷ ʔə ti sʔuladx̌ʷ.   Then he caught another salmon.

gʷəl q̓ʷibidəx̌ʷ.   And he prepared it.

huy, q̓ʷəldax̌ʷ.   Then he cooked it.

14.3a. This clitic represents an obligatory grammatical concept in Lushootseed. Whenever it is appropriate, it must be expressed unlike a number of affixes which are omitted when context would make their inclusion obvious and redundant.

14.3b. Like other clitics and many predicate particles (17.1), ax̌ʷ typically follows the first adverb in a predicate (17.2). (In the example sentences below the adverbs are cickʷ *very*, tiləb *suddenly, bluntly*, x̌ub *should, ought*, and x̌ʷul' *just*. See 17.2 and following.)

cickʷəx̌ʷ t(u)astaq̓ʷuʔ.   He was very thirsty now.

tiləbəx̌ʷ bələq̓x̌ad tsiʔił sʔušəbabdx̌ʷ.   Bluntly now he again insulted that poor dear one.

14.3c. Different from the other clitics but like general prefixes, ax̌ʷ can occur several times in the same predicate (16.1) following both adverb and verb (or other predicate head) and occasionally several adverbs in a row.

x̌ubəx̌ʷ ʔupaq̓atəbəx̌ʷ ʔə ti sʔəłəd.   The food ought to be distributed.

x̌ubəx̌ʷ čəx̌ʷ x̌ʷul'əx̌ʷ łubəščəb.   You should be just a mink.

14.4. The person marking clitics are closely related to the čəd-words in both form and meaning. For easy comparison these two sets of person markers are here presented side by side.

		čəd	ad (əd)
First person	Singular	**čəd**	**ad** (əd)
	Plural	**čəł**	**ałi** (əłi)*
Second person	Singular	**čəx̌ʷ**	**ax̌ʷ** (əx̌ʷ)
	Plural	**čələp**	**aləp** (ələp)
Third person			**as** (əs)

Aside from the vowel difference (because clitics are sometimes stressed (14.2a) but čəd-words never are), the student should find a total of three differences between the above two lists. Two of these differences are specific to this or that particular person marker. The other difference separates one entire set from the other. On the lines below students should describe each difference.

1. _____ .

2. _____ .

3. _____ .

14.4a. Note that the second person singular clitic, axʷ *you*, is homonymous with the aspectual clitic, axʷ *now* (14.3). When both classes of clitics cooccur, the latter precedes the former, e.g., ...gʷəʔux̌ʷəxʷəɬi... *if we go now*, literally, ... *if-go-now-we*.

14.4b. The clitic person markers are used in one type of **subordinate clause**. (Clause types are defined and illustrated in Lesson Twenty-one.) Typically, the verb (or, more precisely, the predicate head) bears the irrealis prefix, ɬu- (13.3/13.4), when the clause expresses what is expected or, at least, anticipated; but it carries the subjunctive prefix, gʷ- (12.3b, 13.4), when the clause conveys doubt or suppositions known to be false, e.g., ...gʷəč'ač'asəd uʔxʷ,[20] ... *if I were still young*.

The following example sentences are a little longer and more varied in meaning than those in previous lessons. Consequently, it is more difficult to determine the gloss of the new words and stems from the English translations. Therefore, a list of words appearing in these lessons for the first time is provided with appropriate glosses.

ʔukʷukʷ* (NL)	play	talə	money
bəsad	darkness, night	stubš	man
č'aʔa* (SL)	play	sťəťtqʷiʔ	drake buffelhead / butterball, *Bucephala albeola*
č'əlpšad	sprain/turn ankle	ťiwiɬ	ask for
sq'ədzuʔ	hair	xʷəƛ'šad	break leg

---

[20]Observe this use (meaning) of the č'ač'as elsewhere glossed as *boy, girl*. The particle uʔxʷ means *still, yet*.

q̓ilid	put [someone/something on board]	x̌əc	afraid
tagʷ-	buy	yayus	work

1. łuxʷakʷʷil čəd ƛ̓uł(u)astagʷəxʷə̲d̲.   I get tired whenever I am hungry.

2. ƛ̓uləcuťilib čəxʷ ʔu łuyayusə̲xʷ̲.   Do you usually sing while you work?

3. ʔuťiwiłtxʷ čəd łuq̓ilidə̲s̲.   I asked [someone] to give [someone else] a ride.[21]

4. ƛ̓uhiił čəł łuʔukʷukʷə̲ł̲i̲.   We are generally happy when we play.

5. łuhikʷ stubš łuluƛ̓ilə̲s̲.   He will be a big man when he grows up.

6. ťukʷ łubəsadə̲s̲.   Come home when it gets dark.

7. ʔəsx̌əc čəd gʷəč̓əlpšadə̲d̲ gʷətəlawilə̲d̲.   I am afraid I would turn [my] ankle if I were to run.

8. haʔł ti sq̓ədᶻuʔ ʔə ti sťəťtqʷiʔ gʷəsq̓ədᶻuʔə̲s̲.   Drake Buffelhead's hair is pretty if it is hair.[22]

9. gʷətagʷš čəxʷ ʔu gʷabstaləhə̲xʷ̲.   Would you buy it if you had [some] money?

10. p̓aƛ̓aƛ̓ dxʷʔal dəgʷi gʷəxʷəƛ̓šadə̲d̲.[23]   It doesn't matter to you if I break a leg.

14.5. Dialect differences. The first person plural of Northern Lushootseed, -ałi, is equivalent to -ał čəł in Southern Lushootseed.

Where Northern Lushootseed has cickʷ *very*, Southern Lushootseed has cay.

---

[21]More literally, I asked [someone] that [he/she] put [someone] on board.

[22]Because the animals of today's world were people in the first world, story tellers sometimes vacillate, as here, between describing them in human or animal terms. Does Drake Buffelhead have feathers or hair on his head? This duality has prompted the concluding clause, *if it is [in fact] hair.*

[23]The main clause in this sentence, p̓aƛ̓aƛ̓ dxʷʔal dəgʷi, involves several grammatical points yet to be presented. Among these is dəgʷi which is still another way of saying *you.* See 19.3.

14.6. Vocabulary comment.

14.6a. The verb tagʷ- *buy* requires -š rather than -d. (See 22.1a, 22.1b.) It can, however, have -alikʷ in place of -š.

14.6b. The word talə *money* entered Lushootseed from Chinook Jargon, the lingua franca of the Pacific Northwest in the Nineteenth and early Twentieth Centuries. However, the Chinook Jargon word came from the English word *dollar*. And from where did the English word come? The student should trace *dollar* to its origin by consulting a good dictionary.

14.7. Exercises.

14.7a. On a separate sheet of paper copy the first eight example sentences of section 14.4b but leave a dash where the stems would go. For example, #1 would be

    ɬu___ čəd ƛuɬ(u)as___əd.

The purpose of this exercise is to impress Lushootseed grammatical structure more firmly upon the student's memory; for when the grammar is mastered, a dictionary is all the student needs to read, write or speak the language.

14.7b. Using the example sentences as a guide, translate the following into Lushootseed on separate paper:

    1. He/she gets tired whenever he/she is hungry.

    2. We usually sing while we work.

    3. Will you be big when you grow up?

    4. I'm afraid to run.

    5. Did she ask for help? (Hint. Use #3 as the model; kʷaxʷad is *help [someone]*.)

    6. You don't care if we fall off. (Hint. Use #10 as the model.)

14.7c. The derivational suffix -šad occurs in two different stems in the example sentences of 14.4b. Write both stems here:

               _____

               _____

What two glosses are given for -šad? _____ and _____.
Specifically, -šad designates the *foot* **and** the *leg* (especially from *below the knee*).

UNIT THREE

CLAUSES AND THEIR STRUCTURE

LESSON FIFTEEN

Demonstratives

15.1. The student is thoroughly familiar with the words ti and tsi, and, at least, acquainted with kʷi and kʷsi. These, however, are only part of a much larger set of words called **demonstratives**. The demonstrative systems (pronominal, adjectival, and adverbial) are complex in Lushootseed for several reasons. They involve a fairly large number of concepts. There is considerable variation among speakers in their use. Finally, adjectival and adverbial demonstratives can enter into a variety of combinations creating still more, and often quite subtle, distinctions than occur in either subclass taken alone.

The basic system, however, is straight forward; and that is what is presented here. The complex and sometimes idiosyncratic combinations are dealt with in footnotes as they occur in the texts.

15.2. Five concepts are marked in the basic adjectival system. These are distal, proximal, unique reference, non-contrastive (or neutral), and hypothetical and/or remote. Each of these can be further marked for feminine. (See, however, 15.2a - 15.2b below.) The specific forms in Northern and Southern Lushootseed differ in several cases.

Adjectival demonstratives

Unmarked

NL	tiʔiɬ	tiʔəʔ	ti	tə	kʷi
SL	tiiɬ	ti	šə	tə	kʷi
	distal	proximal	unique	non-contrastive	hypothetical
	(*that*)	(*this*)	reference	(or neutral)	and/or remote

Marked (feminine)

NL	tsiʔiɬ	tsiʔəʔ	tsi	tsə	kʷsi
SL	tsiiɬ	tsi	sə	tsə	kʷsi

15.2a. The marked forms are used with female referents but only when that referent is singular. One says tsiʔiɬ sɬadəyʔ *that woman* but tiʔiɬ sɬəɬadəyʔ *those women*.

15.2b. Occasionally speakers use the marked form with small animals thereby imparting a notion similar to the English *cute* or *cuddly*. Sometimes, too, the marked form is used with a favourite object, e.g., a canoe, for which the owner feels some sentimental attachment.

15.2c. The unmarked distal and proximal demontratives have augmented (plural) forms, tiʔiʔiɬ and tiʔiʔəʔ. These are never obligatory.

15.2d. Different from English, demonstrative adjectives are used with proper nouns. Lushootseed grammar requires one to say what translates literally as *this Sue* or *the Joe*, etc.

15.2e. Also different from English is the use of demonstratives with nouns inflected for possession, e.g., ti sqʷəbayʔs *the his/her dog*, tsi dskʷuy *the my mother*.

15.2f. In the old stories speakers' selection of the distal or proximal demonstrative with the names of the chief protagonists is based on vague and constantly shifting notions of reference. Often a sentence will paraphrase the one immediately preceding; but the first has tiʔiɬ and the second tiʔəʔ, or visa versa, with negligible or no apparent difference intended by the raconteur.

15.2g. The English demonstrative adjectives *this* and *that* are often inappropriate renditions of tiʔəʔ or tiʔiɬ. In many cases *the*, *a*, or no word at all is more suitable in an English translation of a Lushootseed text. Students should be guided by context and good English style in translating; they should not feel constrained to use *this* or *that* everywhere tiʔəʔ or tiʔiɬ occurs.

15.3. Pronominal demonstratives distinguish only distal from proximal.

Pronominal demonstratives

	Unmarked		Marked (feminine)	
NL	tiʔiɬ	tiʔəʔ	tsiʔiɬ	tsiʔəʔ
SL	tiʔiɬ	ti	tsiʔiɬ	tsi
	distal	proximal	distal	proximal
	(*that*)	(*this*)	(*that*)	(*this*)

Sections 15.2a, 15.2b, 15.2c, and 15.2f apply to these pronouns as well as the demonstrative adjectives.

15.4. Adverbial demonstratives.

tudiʔ/tadiʔ	diʔaʔ*	kʷədiʔ
taʔaʔ	tiʔaʔ	
distal	proximal	remote
(*that*)	(*this*)	

The adverbs in the first row occur in texts far more frequently than taʔaʔ and tiʔaʔ. These second two contrast with tudiʔ/tadiʔ and diʔaʔ by designating a specific spot, e.g., tiʔaʔ *right here* versus diʔaʔ *here*. (Note, however, that the phrase ʔal tiʔaʔ means *around here*.)

15.4a. The forms tudiʔ and tadiʔ are absolute synonyms.

15.4b. Demonstrative adverbs beginning in t- have corresponding marked forms with -s̲-, e.g., tsudiʔ *she over there*, which refer to single female entities as described in 15.2a.[24] A marked form does not exist for diʔaʔ.

15.4c. A reduced form of diʔaʔ *here*, namely diʔəʔ, is very often used by Sauk-Suiattle speakers in phrases with demonstrative adjective and noun, e.g., tiʔəʔ diʔəʔ ʔalʔal *this here house*. (In Lushootseed such phrases carry no social disapproval as does the literal gloss in English.)

15.4d. The first row of demonstrative adverbs is built upon the locative root di(ʔ) *be on/at the side (of)*; and diʔaʔ, tiʔaʔ, and taʔaʔ are derived from the root ʔa(ʔ)/ʔah *be there*.

15.5. Dialect differences. In Southern Lushootseed dišaʔ *here* is used in place of the Northern diʔaʔ.

---

[24]This is probably true of those beginning in kʷ- as well, but the collected texts lack any examples.

15.6. Exercises. Translate the following into Lushootseed.

1. My dog dug up this bone. _____

_____.

2. This girl looked for that. _____.

3. We brought this dog._____.

4. That woman brought us. _____.

5. [Someone] spilled this water. _____.

6. That man took a hold of my dog. _____

_____.

7. Did you folks manage to put the fire out? _____

_____.

8. [Someone] gave a bone to his dog. _____

_____.

LESSON SIXTEEN

Constituents of the clause (parts of the sentence)

16.1. Some Lushootseed sentences have no verbs.[25] Here are a few examples:

1. łubəščəb tiʔił.	That one <u>will become a mink</u>.
2. tusiʔab ti tudsčʼistxʷ.	My former husband <u>was a man of rank</u>.
3. ʔəca ti tudiʔqs.	<u>I am the one</u> who was on the other side of the point.
4. saliʔ tiʔəʔ sqigʷac.	<u>There are two</u> deer.
5. tiʔəʔ tə čʼλaʔ.	<u>This is</u> the rock.
6. tudiʔ tə dukʷibəł.	<u>Way off there is</u> Changer.

In each example the underlined word fills the position usually taken by a verb.[26]

Sometimes it is necessary to refer to the position itself rather than to the class of word that fills it. We shall call this position the **predicate**.

16.2. Other parts of a clause are also named and should now be identified. Different from the predicate however, these other parts are not obligatory. Only the predicate is essential.

16.3. Look again at the first six sentences in Lesson Three. In each of these the first word (which happens to be a verb) fills the predicate position; the remainder is termed the **direct complement**. In these particular sentences the direct complement position is taken by tsi čʼačʼas, ti sʔuladxʷ, and ti sqʷəbayʔ. In the present lesson the part not underlined in 1 through 6 above is the direct complement.

---

[25]A verb is a stem which carries or could carry an aspectual prefix from the list in 11.3c.

[26]Note that the English glosses all require a form of the verb *be* to render these words. Lushootseed lacks a word like *be* (whose function in English is most often little more than a hanger for tense, aspect and person).

16.4. Somewhat peripheral to the core of a clause (i.e., to the predicate plus or minus a direct complement) are three other **constituents** (clause parts). These are the **oblique complement**, one or more **adjuncts** and a locative or temporal **augment**. However, it would be a highly unusual sentence (or more precisely, clause) that had all these constituents. Good Lushootseed style prefers fairly simple syntax packing complexities into the verb morphology instead.

16.5. Oblique complements are that part of the clause which expresses the agent of predicates ending in -t-əb, -du-b, -tu-b, -c-əb, or s-əb.[27] They are always introduced by ʔə and usually follow the predicate but can occur after the direct complement. Review 6.1 and 6.2.

In the following sentence these three constituents (clause parts) are identified:

ʔukʷədatəb	ʔə tiʔəʔ pišpiš	ti sʔuladxʷ.	*The cat took the salmon.*
predicate	oblique	direct	
	complement	complement	

16.6. Augments are single words within the clause which express locative or temporal notions and are not part of any other constituent in the clause. They follow the predicate but are positionally free relative to the other constituents.

In the examples that follow the augments and their glosses are underlined:

tuləʔibəš tiʔił bəščəb <u>liłʔilgʷił</u>.	*Mink was travelling <u>along the shore</u>.*
ʔułəx̌təb <u>dxʷtʼaqʼt</u> dxʷʔal tudiʔ ʔalʔal.	*It was spread <u>up</u> toward yonder house.*

16.7. Whatever remains in the clause is termed the **adjunct**. If a word or phrase is not (part of) the predicate, direct complement, oblique complement, or augment, it is (a part of) an adjunct.

16.7a. Before discussing the adjunct, it is convenient to introduce the terms ʔə-**phrase** and ʔal-**phrase**. These are simply complements introduced by ʔə, ʔal, or in the latter case, by one of its derivatives, dxʷʔal, tulʔʔal, or lilʔʔal. These phrases remind English speakers of prepositional phrases and students may find it useful to think of them as such. The most frequent glosses for ʔal-phrases are the following:

---

[27]There are two anomalous cases, tagʷib *bought* from tagʷš (14.6a) and x̌ʼalib *worn* from x̌ʼalš *put (clothing) on*. The expected forms *tagʷtəb and *x̌ʼaltəb do not exist.

ʔal   in, on, at, when

dxʷʔal[28]   toward, until, in order to, the reason for

tulʼʔal   from

liɬʔal   by way of, by means of, source, cause

16.7b. Here follow several examples of each:

ʔutəč <u>ʔal</u> tiʔiɬ x̌ɬidup.	It rolled <u>on</u> the floor.
ʔubəčatəb tiʔəʔ sdəxʷiɬ <u>ʔal</u> tiʔiɬ x̌ʷəlč.	[Someone] set the hunting canoe <u>in</u> the water.
ʔuyayus <u>ʔal</u> tiʔəʔ ʔalʔal.	[Someone] worked <u>in</u> the house.
ʔuʔəɬəd əlgʷə <u>ʔal</u> ti təbu.	They eat <u>at</u> the table.
ʔəstʼigʷid <u>ʔal</u> kʷi dadatut.	Thank [someone] <u>in</u> the morning.[29]
ləscil tiʔiɬ jəsəds <u>ʔal</u> tiʔiɬ səʔibəšs.	Her feet go along supported <u>when</u> she walks.
cickʷ siʔab tsiʔəʔ kʼaʔkʼaʔ <u>ʔal</u>əxʷ kʷi tusəshuys ʔaciɬtalbixʷ.	Crow was very high class <u>when</u> she was made as a human.
ɬuqəɫc čəxʷ <u>ʔal</u> kʷi ɬuʔɬp, <u>ʔal</u> tqačiʔ.	Wake me up a little early, <u>at</u> eight.
ɬutəlawil čəd <u>dxʷʔal</u> ti xʷuyubalʔtxʷ.	I'll run <u>to</u> the store.
dəgʷaš <u>dxʷʔal</u> tə xʷdəgʷigʷsali.	Put [something] <u>into</u> the bag.
ʔuɬəx̌təb dxʷtʼaq̓t <u>dxʷʔal</u> tudiʔ ʔalʔal.	It was spread up <u>toward</u> yonder house.
ʔuxʷəbtəb <u>dxʷʔal</u> x̌ʷəlč.	[Someone] was thrown <u>into</u> the sea.
ʔudxʷidawligʷəd čəd <u>dxʷʔal</u> tiʔiɬ tə q̓iɬʼbid.	I'm worried <u>about</u> the car.
ɬ(u)asʔaʔsil čəd <u>dxʷʔal</u> kʷi ƛʼagʷt.	I'll wait <u>until</u> noon.
ʔukʷədatəb ʔə tə sqʷəbayʔ ti šaw <u>tulʼʔal</u> tə čawəyʔulč*.	The dog took the bone <u>from</u> the dish.
ʔubapadəxʷ čəd <u>tulʼʔal</u> ti syayus(s).	I distracted [someone] <u>from</u> his/her work.

---

[28]Always dxʷʔal is pronounced as though spelled txʷəl.

[29]This is the Lushootseed translation of the lyrics to the Christian hymn *Praise Him in the Morning*.

ləslilcut čəd <u>tul'ʔal</u> kʷi bək̓ʷ sp'aƛ̓aƛ̓ ʔal ti swatixʷtəd.	I am keeping myself <u>from</u> all the worthlessness in the world.
ʔəstⁿildxʷ čəd <u>tul'ʔal</u> bək̓ʷ dsptidgʷasəb.	I believe it <u>with</u> all my thoughts.
ʔiⁿ(h)aʔⁿ <u>tul'ʔal</u> kʷi x̌ʷiʔ.	It is better <u>than</u> nothing.
ⁿutulil* <u>liⁿʔaⁿ</u> x̌ʷəlč dxʷʔal d̓id̓əlal 'ič.	[Someone] will go <u>by</u> sea to Seattle.
ləsq'il čəd <u>liⁿʔal</u> ti lilud.	I am travelling <u>by</u> train.
ləsƛ'agʷt čəd <u>liⁿʔal</u> tə stiqiw.	I'm riding <u>on</u> the horse.
ʔucⁿil <u>liⁿʔal</u> tə qədxʷs.	[Someone] bleeds <u>through</u> his/her mouth.
ləskʷax̌ʷac čəx̌ʷ <u>liⁿʔal</u> tiʔiⁿ haʔⁿ adsptidgʷasəb.	You are helping me <u>by</u> your good thoughts.

16.7c. In form ʔə-phrases are like ʔal-phrases; but ʔal and its derivatives have meaning in their own right which they bring to the adjunct they fill, whereas ʔə has no lexical import. Its presence is simply required by Lushootseed grammar.[30]

The ʔə-phrases serve several grammatical roles in Lushootseed three of which have already been learned.

(1)   They fill oblique complements (16.5) thereby providing for the expression of agents for predicates ending in -təb, -dub, -tub, -cəb, and -səb.

(2)   They relate possessor to item possessed (12.3d).

(3)   They designate the patient of a subclass of agent oriented verbs (7.1 - 7.1b, *ff.*).

(At this point the student should review 7.1b - 7.6.)

These three functions, plus the others to be presented later, all have in common the addition of supplemental information. Specifically, ʔə-phrases are used to add to a clause any role not specified by predicate suffixes or an ʔal-phrase; they are used when nothing else is available. Here are several diverse examples:

| ʔupusutəb <u>ʔə ti č̓ač̓as</u> tiʔəʔ sqʷəbayʔ | <u>ʔə tə č̓x̌aʔ</u>. | <u>The boy</u> threw at the dog |
| agent | instrument | <u>with a rock</u>. |

---

[30]Compare the similarly meaningless *to* in an English sentence such as *I like to swim.* It adds no content, no 'dictionary' meaning to the sentence. Its presence is simply required by English grammar.

ʔuyayus	ʔə tə tib.	[Someone] worked <u>hard</u>.
	adverbial phrase	
ʔuʔəɬəd	ʔə tə biac.	[Someone] ate <u>the meat</u>.
	patient	

16.8. Adjuncts are filled with either an ʔal-phrase or an ʔə-phrase. However, not all such phrases are adjuncts. Very occasionally speakers construe an ʔal-phrase as a predicate and, as just pointed out, some ʔə-phrases fill oblique complements and some mark possessive relationships within a complement (12.3d).

16.9. Since some adjuncts are filled by ʔə-phrases and it is an ʔə-phrase that fills the oblique complement, the student may wonder why a distinction is made between oblique complement and adjunct. The explanation is most easily understood by comparing the paraphrases of two clauses, one with an oblique complement, the other with an adjunct:

ʔugʷəč'təb	ʔə tiʔəʔ sqʷəbayʔ. : sqʷəbayʔ tiʔəʔ ʔugʷəč'əd.	*The dog looked for*
	oblique	*[something].*
	complement	
ʔugʷəč'əb	ʔə tiʔəʔ sqʷəbayʔ. : sqʷəbayʔ tiʔəʔ sugʷəč'əbs.	*[Someone] looked for*
	adjunct	*the dog.*

In both cases the paraphrases to the right focus on sqʷəbayʔ more directly than in the sentences on the left. This difference is discussed in Lessons Nineteen and Twenty. To be noted here, however, is the added inflection, namely, s- ... -s, carried by ʔugʷəč'əb when sqʷəbayʔ from the <u>adjunct</u> <u>is</u> <u>initial</u>. No such added inflection is required when sqʷəbayʔ from the <u>oblique</u> <u>complement</u> <u>is</u> <u>initial</u>. (However, -təb must be replaced by -(ə)d.)

These differences between the paraphrases reveal a clear difference between adjuncts and oblique complements -- one that is disguised by the fact that both constituents are expressed by ʔə-phrases.

16.10. Vocabulary comment. The word for *store*, xʷuyubalʔtxʷ, is derived from the word for *sell, trade* plus the suffix -alʔtxʷ *house, building*. This suffix belongs to a very large class of word-building endings called **lexical suffixes**. There are about one hundred of these in Lushootseed.

Similarly, the word for *dish*, č'awəyʔulč, is composed of č'awəyʔ *shell* and the lexical suffix -ulč *container*.

The word xʷdəgʷigʷsali *bag, pocket* is derived from sdəgʷigʷs *paraphernalia* by the addition of the lexical suffix -ali *place where* and the derivational prefix xʷ-. In turn, sdəgʷigʷs is composed of a root dəgʷ (from dəkʷ *inside*) plus the lexical suffix -igʷs *things, possessions* and the derivational prefix s-.

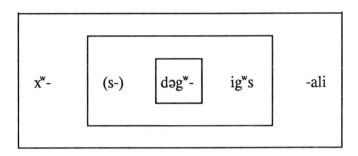

Such layered word building is typical in Lushootseed.

16.11. Dialect differences. The Southern Lushootseed say čuwəyʔulč instead of čawəyʔulč.

The Skagit say šaq̓il *cross a body of water* instead of tulil.

16.12. Exercises. The constituents (clause parts) of the sentences below have been separated from each other by extra spaces. The student is to label each constituent appropriately on the blanks provided and then translate the entire sentence on the following line.

1. ʔuɫəx̌təb   dxʷt'aq̓t   dxʷʔal tudiʔ ʔalʔal.

    _____   _____   _____

    _____.

2. ʔupusutəb   ʔə ti čačas   tiʔəʔ sqʷəbayʔ   ʔə ti čƛ̓aʔ.

    _____   _____   _____   _____

    _____.

3. ləʔibəš   ʔal tiʔəʔ liɫʔilgʷiɫ ʔə tə x̌ʷəlč.

    _____   _____

    _____.

4. ləʔibəš   liɬʔilgʷiɬ.

_____ _____

_____.

5. tiʔəʔ   tə čƛ̓aʔ.

_____ _____

_____.

6. ʔukʷədatəb   ʔə tiʔəʔ pišpiš.

_____ _____

_____.

7. ʔupusutəb   ʔə ti čƛ̓aʔ.

_____ _____

_____.

8. ʔukʷədatəb   tiʔəʔ pišpiš.

_____ _____

_____.

9. ʔuʔabyitəb   ʔə ti luƛ̓   ʔə ti sqʷəbayʔ.

_____ _____ _____

_____.

10.   ʔuʔəɬəd   ʔə ti bəsqʷ.

_____ _____

_____.

11.   ʔuqʷʔəld   ti sʔuladxʷ.

_____ _____

_____.

12.   ʔuʔabyitəb   ti čačas   ʔə ti sqʷəbayʔ.

_____ _____ _____

_____.

13.   ʔuqʷʔəlb   ʔə ti sʔuladxʷ.

_____ _____

_____.

14.   ʔučʼaʔəb   tsi sɬadəyʔ   ʔə tə skʷʼiʔxʷ   ʔal tudiʔ.

_____ _____ _____ _____

_____.

LESSON SEVENTEEN

Predicate and complement structure; predicate particles and adverbs

The student is now familiar with predicates and various complements. The present lesson first details the ways that predicates can be "enlarged" with particles (17.1, 17.3) and adverbs (17.2, 17.3) to enrich their meaning. Then the potential structure of complements is presented beginning with 17.4.

17.1. Compare and contrast the following six sentences with one another:

1. ʔəsx̌əɫ		tsiʔəʔ k̓aʔk̓aʔ.	Crow is sick.
2. ʔəsx̌əɫ	uʔx̌ʷ	tsiʔəʔ k̓aʔk̓aʔ.	Crow is still sick.
3. ʔəsx̌əɫ	dᶻəɫ	tsiʔəʔ k̓aʔk̓aʔ.	Crow must be sick.
4. ʔəsx̌əɫ	k̓ʷəɫ	tsiʔəʔ k̓aʔk̓aʔ.	They say Crow is sick.
5. ʔəsx̌əɫ	əw̓ə	tsiʔəʔ k̓aʔk̓aʔ.	So, Crow is sick. (Mild surprise.)
6. ʔəsx̌əɫ	six̌ʷ	tsiʔəʔ k̓aʔk̓aʔ.	Crow is sick as usual! (Mild disgust.)

17.1a. Each one of the words within the box is called **a predicate particle**. Many such particles, as do most of the above, convey various attitudes of the speaker, but there are others which are purely grammatical. These latter include the čəd-words and the interrogative ʔu.

17.1b. Predicate particles can cooccur. Here are a few examples:

7. ʔəsx̌əɫ <u>uʔx̌ʷ</u> čəx̌ʷ <u>ʔu</u>.	Are you still sick?
8. ʔəs(h)əliʔtub <u>uʔx̌ʷ</u> <u>dᶻəɫ</u> <u>čəx̌ʷ</u>.	You must still be kept alive.
9. ʔəsx̌əɫ <u>six̌ʷ</u> <u>dᶻəɫ</u> <u>əw̓ə</u> tsiʔəʔ k̓aʔk̓aʔ.[31]	It seems Crow must be sick.
10. ʔəsx̌əɫ <u>k̓ʷəɫ</u> <u>əw̓ə</u> <u>dᶻəɫ</u> <u>ʔu</u> <u>six̌ʷ</u> tsi k̓aʔk̓aʔ.	So, does it seem that Crow is sick as usual as they say?

---

[31]This sentence drips sarcasm.

17.1c. Comparing the positions of these particles relative to one another in sentences 9 and 10 shows that their order is to some extent significant. However, čəd-words always occur before ʔu, and uʔxʷ precedes both. Furthermore, certain arrangements are more frequent than others. For example, kʷəɬ tends to follow the verb before the others while sixʷ is typically the last predicate particle in a string. Part of the effect in 9 above is achieved by having sixʷ before all the other particles.

17.2. Predicate adverbs precede the verb.

11. <u>cickʷ</u> ʔəstagʷəxʷ tiʔəʔ qawʼqs.   Raven is <u>very</u> hungry.

12. <u>ckʷaqid</u> ʔəstagʷəxʷ tiʔəʔ qawʼqs.   Raven is <u>always</u> hungry.

13. <u>tiləbəxʷ</u>[32] ʔusaxʷəb tiʔiɬ bəščəb.   Mink <u>immediately</u> ran.

14. <u>x̌ʷulʼ</u> ʔuʔəɬəd tiʔəʔ qawʼqs.   Raven <u>just</u> eats.

17.2a. Some Lushootseed words are exclusively predicate adverbs such as the four examples immediately above. This group has ten members:

cickʷ (NL)	very	gʷaʔxʷ	eventually, soon
cay (SL)	very	put	very much so, in a great way
ckʷaqid	always	tiləb	immediately, bluntly; right there
daʔxʷ / dawʼ	just now	x̌əɬ ti	as though, like
dəxʷ	(meaning unknown)	x̌ʷulʼ	just (that and nothing else)

Other words, however, can fill a variety of lexical categories only one of which is that of a predicate adverb. This group has about sixteen members or so.

bəkʷ	all	hiqab	excessively, too (much)
cəɬulʼ	previously, in advance	λ̕alʼ	also, too
cukʷ / cugʷ- (Sk)	only, uniquely	λ̕ub	well; ought, should
dayʼ (Snoh., SL)	only, uniquely, separate, isolated; foremost, especially; completely, all		
gʷəhawʼə	it seems	tux̌ʷ	in contrast to the usual or expected

---

[32]For the əxʷ ending on tiləb, see 14.3 (and 14.2a, 17.3).

haʔkʷ / hagʷ-	ago, long time	xʷɬub	ultimately, in fact
haʔɬ	well, good	xʷiʔ	no, not
(hə)laʔb	really, a lot	xʷuʔələʔ	maybe, perhaps
hikʷ	big, very	yawʼ	only if, not until

17.2b. Sequences of adverbs occur. Here are a few examples:

15. <u>cickʷ</u> <u>həlaʔb</u> ʔəsqad tiʔiɬ stiqiw.   That horse is <u>really</u> <u>very</u> slow.

16. <u>cickʷ</u> <u>xʷuʔələʔ</u> <u>həlaʔb</u> ʔəsx̌əɬ   He is <u>really</u> <u>very</u> sick <u>I guess</u>.
    tiʔiɬ.

17. x̌ʼubəxʷ <u>x̌ʷulʼəxʷ</u> ɬubəščəb.   It <u>is</u> <u>better</u> that he become <u>just</u> a mink.

17.3. When both particles and adverbs occur in the same predicate, the particle or sequence of particles follows the adverb instead of the verb.

18. cickʷ <u>čəd</u> ʔəxʷʔux̌ʷəb.   I very [much] want to go.

19. hikʷ <u>čəxʷ</u> <u>ʔu</u> x̌ʼux̌əɬqid.   Do you generally get severe headaches?

20. dayʼəxʷ <u>əwʼə</u> <u>six̌ʷ</u> ʔusaʔil tiʔəʔ   Raven really stuck his foot in it this time.[33]
    qawʼqs.

17.3a. When there is more than one adverb in the predicate, grammatical particles follow the first adverb.

21. dayʼəxʷ <u>čəd</u> cickʷ ʔəslaqil.   Indeed, I am very late.

22. x̌ʼub <u>čəɬ</u> <u>ʔu</u> x̌ʷulʼ ɬuʔukʷ.   Should we just go home?

17.3b. Typically, predicate particles expressing the speaker's attitude also follow the first adverb.

23. dayʼəxʷ <u>dᶻəɬ</u> higʷəxʷ   Indeed, [someone] must have spilled all
    ʔukʷəɬkʷɬatəb ti tudqʷuʔ.   my water.

24. ckʷaqid <u>six̌ʷ</u> x̌ʷulʼ ʔuʔəɬəd tiʔəʔ   Raven is always just eating.
    qawʼqs.

---

[33]More literally, 'So, indeed, Raven got into trouble again.'

However, the location of these particles of emotion is to some extent determined by meaning. Speakers have the option of using the particle with one or another adverb.

25. cickʷ ƛ̌ʷəɬ xʷuʔələʔ hələʔb   So, I guess they say that Crow is really very
    əwʼə ʔəsx̌əɬ tsiʔəʔ k̓aʔk̓aʔ.   sick.

26. cickʷ xʷuʔələʔ sixʷ hələʔb   I guess Raven is really very hungry again.
    ʔəstagʷəxʷ tiʔəʔ qawʼqs.

17.4. Potentially, complement structures are more complex than predicates but typically they too are quite simple. In its simplest and most frequent form a complement comprises a pronoun[34] or a demonstrative plus noun. The student is thoroughly familiar with complements like tiʔiɬ *that (one)*, ti sqʷəbayʔ *the dog* and tsiʔəʔ sɬadəyʔ *this woman*.

17.4a. Occasionally complements are expanded by modifiers resulting in phrases reminiscent of English noun phrases of the form determiner + adjective + noun, and determiner + adverb + adjective + noun.

tiʔəʔ hik̓ʷ ʔalʔal   this <u>big</u> house

tiʔiɬ luX̌ x̌payʔac   that <u>old</u> cedar tree

ti hələʔb haʔɬ səplil   the <u>really good</u> bread

17.4b. A word from any class can modify a noun in this way including verbs as embedded predicates and other nouns. (Compare 21.6c.)

tiʔəʔ ʔəstʼiq̓ʷilabac stubš   this <u>covered with sores</u> man

tiʔiɬ x̌ʷiʔ ləhaʔɬ bəščəb   that <u>no good</u> mink

tiʔəʔ haʔɬ ʔuk̓ʷikʷʼəɬ q̓ʷuʔ   This <u>nice trickling</u> water

tiʔəʔ kiyuuq̓ʷs stətudəq   these <u>seagull</u> slaves

tiʔəʔ diʔəʔ ɬixʷixʷ čačʼas stububš   these (here) <u>three young</u> men

tiʔəʔ ʔiɬt̓isu bədaʔs   his/her <u>youngest</u> son

---

[34]The only pronouns presented thus far are pronominal demonstratives in 15.3 and the words ʔəca *I (am the one)* in example sentence 3 of 16.1 and dəgʷi *you (are the one)* in example sentence 10 of 14.4b. See also 19.3.

17.4c. Predicates and nouns can also follow the words they modify.

tiʔəʔ stubš ʔəstʼiqʷilabac	this man covered with sores
ti stubš čʼačʼas	the man [who is] <u>young</u>
tiʔəʔ bədaʔs ʔiɬtʼisu	his/her son [who is the] <u>youngest</u>

17.4d. Sequences of nouns of the sort exemplified immediately above are distinct from the following cases where one noun is in **apposition** to another.

tiʔiɬ tətyiqaʔ, <u>suʔsuqʷaʔs</u>	Tutyeekah, <u>his little younger brother</u>
tiʔəʔ tusčʼistxʷs, <u>tuḏiyax̌əd</u>	her former husband, <u>former Slug</u>
tsiʔəʔ čəgʷas(s), <u>tsiʔəʔ x̌ʷuʔx̌ʷəyʔ</u>	his wife, <u>Little Diver</u>
tiʔiɬ taʔtəmi, <u>haʔɬ sčʼačʼas čəɬ</u>	Tommy, <u>our good youngster</u>

17.4e. Complements can also be expanded by compounding.

tuhuycut <u>tiʔəʔ qawʼqs ʔi* tiʔəʔ bibščəb</u>.	<u>Raven and Little Mink</u> prepared themselves.
ʔəsɬaɬlil tiʔiɬ <u>ʔi sgʷəlub ʔi tiʔəʔ qawʼqs</u>.	They were dwelling [there], <u>both Pheasant and Raven</u>.
…<u>tsiʔəʔ kʼaʔkʼaʔ ʔi tiʔəʔ kiyuuqs(s)</u>.	… <u>Crow and her seagulls</u>.

17.4f. Still another means of expanding a complement is by means of ʔə- and ʔal-phrases.

tsiʔəʔ čəgʷas <u>ʔə tiʔəʔ sgʷəlub</u>	the wife <u>of Pheasant</u>
tiʔiɬ bədbədaʔ <u>ʔə tiʔiɬ qawʼqs</u>	those children <u>of Raven</u>
tiʔiɬ səxʷgʷədil* <u>ʔal tiʔiɬ tibu</u>	that chair <u>by that table</u>

17.4g. Occasionally the entire complement is itself modified as in the following example. Here the inherently stative (10.4) bəkʷ *all* is outside but modifies tiʔəʔ ḏilʼbids əlgʷəʔ.

ʔəsčadʼil <u>bəkʷ</u> tiʔəʔ ḏilʼbids əlgʷəʔ.	They are hiding [themselves] <u>including</u> their canoe.

17.5. Dialect differences.

17.5a. The conjunction ʔi is Northern Lushootseed. The equivalent form in Southern Lushootseed is yəxʷ.

17.5b. The Skagit say x̌ʷt'agʷtap for *chair* while other groups say səxʷgʷədil.

17.6. Exercises. Rearrange the following sets of words into a grammatically acceptable order for a Lushootseed predicate. Provide an English translation for each set.

1. ʔu, ʔəsx̌əɬ, čəxʷ: _____.

   Translation: _____.

2. ʔu, ʔəsx̌əɬ, čəxʷ, həlaʔb: _____.

   Translation: _____.

3. ʔuʔəɬəd, ckʷʼaqid, sixʷ, x̌ʷul': _____.

   Translation: _____.

4. ʔu, ʔəsx̌əɬ, uʔxʷ, čəxʷ: _____.

   Translation: _____.

5. ʔu, čəɬ, ɬuƛ'ukʷ, ƛub, x̌ʷul': _____.

   Translation: _____.

LESSON EIGHTEEN

Negatives

The following four brief conversations present three different negative statements, two of which are grammatically very similar and a third which is quite different. The student should study these conversations carefully and then identify each pattern by creating one negative statement representing each type with the vocabulary provided below.

Speaker A:	1. ʔah ʔu kʷi gʷadpišpiš.	Do you have a cat?
Speaker B:	2. xʷiʔ kʷi gʷədpišpiš.	I don't have a cat.
	3. xʷiʔ kʷi gʷəpišpiš ʔal tiʔaʔ.	There are no cats around here.
Speaker A:	4. gʷəl stab əw'ə tiʔəʔ.	Then, what's this?
Speaker B:	5. xʷiʔ ləpišpiš tiʔił.	That's not a cat.
	6. sq'əbiyəʔ tiʔił!	That's a skunk!

Speaker A:	1. ʔah ʔu kʷi gʷadsqʷəbayʔ.	Do you have a dog?
Speaker B:	2. xʷiʔ kʷi gʷədsqʷəbayʔ.	I don't have a dog.
	3. xʷiʔ kʷi gʷəsqʷəbayʔ ʔal tiʔaʔ.	There are no dogs around here.
Speaker A:	4. gʷəl stab əw'ə tiʔił.	Then, what's that?
Speaker B:	5. xʷiʔ ləsqʷəbayʔ tiʔił.	That's not a dog.
	6. sbiaw tiʔił.	That's a coyote.

Speaker A:	1. kʷid kʷi gʷadscqi.	How many sockeye do you have?
Speaker B:	2. xʷiʔ kʷi gʷədscqi.	I don't have [any] sockeye,
	3. yəxi xʷiʔ ləscqi tiʔiʔəʔ.	because these are not sockeye.
	4. xʷiʔ kʷi gʷəscqi ʔal tiʔəʔ stuləkʷ.	There are no sockeye in this river.
	5. x̌'xʷayʔ tiʔiʔəʔ sʔuladxʷ.	These salmon are chum.
	6. ʔah tiʔəʔ buus.	There are four.

Speaker A:	1. stab tiʔił ʔal ti ʔilgʷił.	What is that on the shore?
Speaker B:	2. qaw'qs tiʔił.	That's a raven.

Speaker C: 3. xʷiʔ ləqawʼqs.   It's not a raven.
            4. kʼaʔkʼaʔ tiʔił.   That's a crow.
            5. ləliʔ kʼi bəqsəd ʔə kʼi qawʼqs.   The beak of a raven is different.

With the word čʼəx̌bidac *yew tree* create the following sentences:

1. That is not a yew tree. _____.

2. There are no yew trees around here. _____.

3. We do not have [any] yew trees. _____.

18.1.   Negatives were first presented in Lesson Twelve.   These were <u>negatives of</u> <u>existence</u>. (The student should reread the example sentences 1a through 3c in Lesson Twelve and 12.3 through 12.3c.) In such sentences xʷiʔ (like ʔah *there*, qah *many, much, a lot*, and a small number of other high frequency words) is the predicate and what follows is the direct complement. (But compare 18.6a.)

Negatives of existence correspond to two rather different formations in English. Note carefully the difference between sentences numbered 2 and those numbered 3 in the first three dialogues above. For convenience the first set is repeated here:

  2. xʷiʔ kʼi gʷədpišpiš.   I don't have a cat.

  3. xʷiʔ kʼi gʷəpišpiš . . .   There are no cats . . .

In Lushootseed the only difference between them is the presence of a d-paradigm in 2 lacking in 3. The English glosses suggest a greater dissimilarity than is required.

18.2.   Negative sentences of the form xʷiʔ lə . . . are <u>negatives of identity</u>. In these formations xʷiʔ is an adverb and lə is a **proclitic** going on the next adverb. If there is no other adverb, lə attaches to the head word (main word) in the predicate.[35] (Note that this lə is not to be confused with the progressive prefix, lə- (11.3b).)

18.3.   The same distinction between the predicate xʷiʔ and the adverb xʷiʔ obtains in the sentences expressing activities. Compare the following conversations.

---

[35]Compare the position of lə in the predicate with that of the clitics (14.3b).

Speaker A:	1. xʷiʔtxʷ ləgʷuub tiʔiɬ adsqʷəbayʔ.	Don't let your dog bark.
Speaker B:	2. xʷiʔ lədsgʷaʔ tiʔiɬ sqʷəbayʔ tiʔiɬ ləcugʷuub.	It's not my dog that's barking.
	3. adsgʷaʔ.	It's yours.
	4. haʔɬ ti dsqʷəbayʔ.	My dog is good.
	5. xʷiʔ kʷi gʷəsugʷuubs.	He doesn't bark.

Speaker A:	1. xʷiʔtxʷ ləx̌aab tiʔiɬ adbibədaʔ.	Don't let your little boy cry.
Speaker B:	2. xʷiʔ lədsgʷaʔ tiʔiɬ bibədaʔ tiʔiɬ ləcux̌aab.	That's not my little boy who's crying.
	3. adsgʷaʔ.	[He's] yours.
	4. haʔɬ ti dbibədaʔ.	My little boy is good.
	5. xʷiʔ kʷi gʷəsux̌aabs.	He doesn't cry.

Speaker A:	1. ckʷaqid čəd x̌ubaliic kʷi gʷədsuʔəɬtxʷ ti dsqʷəbayʔ.	I always forget to feed my dog.
	2. xʷiʔtubš ləbəbaliic ʔal kʷi dadatut.	Don't let me forget again to-morrow.
Speaker B:	3. x̌ub.	OK.

Speaker A:	1. xʷiʔtxʷ ləʔəx̌ʼ əlgʷəʔ.	Don't let them come.
	2. xʷiʔ kʷi gʷəsuc'agʷacuts əlgʷəʔ.	They don't wash themselves.
	3. sʔm hmmmm!	Phew!
Speaker B:	4. (Shocked silence.)	

18.4. When the speaker's chief attention is on the negation, xʷiʔ-predicates are used. These times include strong prohibitions (negative commands like *Do not . . .*) and statements denying an activity, i.e., *does not*.

18.5. When the activity is still paramount in the speaker's mind, the negation is formed with the adverb plus lə. Most such cases involve negative exhortations.

18.6. Note that čəd-words are used in negatives formed with the adverbial xʷiʔ while d-paradigm affixes are used in predicate-xʷiʔ sentences.

18.6a. Furthermore, this second negative type also requires that a verb bear the s-prefix. (This is different from negated noun stems which carry an s-prefix only if they belong to the s-prefix class.) In other words, verbs negated by predicate-xʷiʔ are **nominalized**. (See 21.5.)

18.6b. The sentences below are partially diagrammed to show the two types of negation presented in this lesson.

xʷiʔ	čəxʷ	sixʷ	ləbakʷɫ.	Don't get hurt again.
adverb	particle	particle	predicate head
< ————————— predicate ————— >

xʷiʔ	kʷi	gʷ-ad-s-u-ʔəɬəd.	You did not eat.
		nominalized
		verb stem
< –predicate — >	< — direct complement — >

18.7. The suffix -txʷ bound to the negative adverb, xʷiʔ, is the same suffix encountered in Lesson One, the causative. How would one say in Lushootseed, *Don't let me cry*?

18.8. Exercises. On a separate sheet of paper translate the following into English by using the glossary that accompanies the texts:

1. xʷiʔ kʷi gʷadsʔuxʷʔ.
2. xʷiʔ lədiɬ.
3. xʷiʔ ləhəlaʔb sʔəɬəd.
4. xʷiʔ kʷədaʔ kʷi gʷəsqəlbs.
5. xʷiʔtubš čəxʷ ləxʷitʼil.
6. xʷiʔ kʷi gʷədtalə.
7. xʷiʔ ləhəlaʔb qa(h) ti dsuʔəɬəd.
8. xʷiʔ lədsgʷaʔ.

LESSON NINETEEN

Focus of agent and patient

Contrast the following two English sentences:

The youngsters chased the dog.

The dog is what the youngsters chased.

They impart the same information but the second, in contrast to the first, **focuses** on *dog*.

All languages have techniques for focusing. In this lesson and the one following, the grammar of Lushootseed focusing is presented.

19.1. In Lushootseed as in many languages focusing is achieved by stating the focused material first. Compare what follows to this relatively neutral statement:

ʔučalatəb ʔə tiʔiɬ wiw̓su tiʔəʔ sq̉ʷəbayʔ.   *The children chased the dog.*

When the speaker elects to focus attention on the direct complement (16.3), filled in this case by tiʔəʔ sq̉ʷəbayʔ, the head word sq̉ʷəbayʔ (with or without the adjectival demonstrative (15.2)) is stated first AND the original predicate (16.1) is preceded by a demonstrative word (15.1). All else is unchanged as in this sentence:

sq̉ʷəbayʔ ti ʔučalatəb ʔə tiʔiɬ wiw̓su.   *A dog is what the children chased.*

One could also say, tiʔəʔ sq̉ʷəbayʔ ti ʔučalatəb ʔə tiʔiɬ wiw̓su. The adjectival demonstrative, tiʔəʔ, is optional with the focused sq̉ʷəbayʔ, but a demonstrative (ti in this case) is required before the original predicate, ʔučalatəb in this sentence.

19.2. If, instead, the speaker intends to focus on the oblique complement 16.5), the head word of that constituent (clause part) comes first. As with focused direct complements, so too with oblique complements, the original predicate must be preceded by a demonstrative. Also, the -(ə)b of -t-əb, -du-b, -tu-b, -c-əb, and -s-əb cannot be maintained because there is no longer an explicit or implicit oblique complement following the verb. Contrast the two sentences in 19.1 with the following:

wiw̓su tiʔəʔ ʔučalad tiʔəʔ sq̉ʷəbayʔ.   *The children are the ones who chased the dog.*

19.3. When the speaker focuses on a person marker (which the student will remember corresponds to an English pronoun), special words are used. Some of these are listed here.

ʔəca	*I am the one.*	dibəɬ	*We are the ones.*
dəgʷi	*You are the one.*	gʷəlap(u)	*You folks are the ones.*
cədiɬ	*He, she, it, that is the one.*	caadiɬ	*They are the ones.*

Two example sentences are these:

ʔəca tiʔəʔ ləčalad tə sqʷəbayʔ.	*I am the one who is chasing the dog.*
dəbəɬ ti ʔuƛ'uc'utəb ʔə tiʔiɬ šəbad.	*We are the ones who were shot by the enemy.*

19.4. The words ʔəca, dibəɬ, dəgʷi, gʷəlap(u), cədiɬ, and a few others such as gʷat *who* and diɬ *that, he, she, it* are full words as opposed to particles, clitics, or affixes, and as such they sometimes head predicates as well as both types of complements and adjuncts. In addition to focus, they are used for a variety of emphatic nuances.

19.5. Interrogative words such as gʷat *who, whom* and stab *what* are inherently focusing by virtue of their meanings. The grammar of questions formed with these words is just like the preceding sentences with focused agents and patients; here too a demonstrative precedes the predicate.

19.5a. When the interrogative asks about a direct complement, the questions formed are like the second one in 19.1:

(tiʔəʔ) sqʷəbayʔ ti ʔučalatəb ʔə tiʔiɬ wiwʼsu.	This dog is the one the children chased.
<u>gʷat</u> kʷi ʔuʔəyʼdub ʔə ti sqʷəbayʔ.	Whom did the dog find?
<u>stab</u> kʷi ʔuʔəyʼdub ʔə ti sqʷəbayʔ.	What did the dog find?

19.5b. When the interrogative word asks about an oblique complement, the questions take the same form as statements like those in 19.2:

wiwʼsu tiʔəʔ ʔučalad tiʔəʔ sqʷəbayʔ.	The children are the ones who chased the dog.
ʔəca tiʔəʔ ləčalad tə sqʷəbayʔ.	I am the one who is chasing the dog.

gʷat kʷi ʔuʔəy'dxʷ ti sqʷəbayʔ.	Who found the dog?
stab kʷi ʔux̌əƛ̌əd ti sqʷəbayʔ?	What bit the dog?

19.6. To this point all examples in this lesson have been sentences in which both agent and patient are third persons (12.5). When either the agent or the patient is first or second person (12.5), the questions are formed in an equally straight forward manner.

19.6a. Interrogative words representing the agent:

gʷat kʷi gʷək̓ʷax̌ʷac̣.	Who can help me?
gʷat kʷi gʷəʔəɬtubuɬəd.	Who would feed you folks?
stab kʷi ʔux̌əcdubicid.	What scared you?

19.6b. Interrogative words representing the patient:

gʷat kʷi gʷək̓ʷax̌ʷad čəd.	Whom can I help?
gʷat kʷi ʔuʔəɬtxʷ čələp.	Whom did you folks feed?
stab kʷi ʔuʔəy'dxʷ čəxʷ.	What did you find?

19.7. By far the most frequently used of these focus words is diɬ *the one(s) mentioned before, the one(s) about to be mentioned, that (which)*. The grammar involved with diɬ is the same as with other focused expressions in all respects except one. Speakers often omit the demonstrative (15.1, 15.2) that obligatorily follows other focus expressions. In the four texts of this introductory reader the expected demonstrative is always lacking.

diɬ shuys. 2.66, 4.99	That is finished/completed.
diɬ sc̓əldxʷs. 3.76	That is how he managed to win.
diɬ dəxʷut̓asad čəɬ tiʔəʔ č̓x̌aʔ. 3.11	That is why we pay this rock.
diɬ day̓ ƛ̓uscut ʔə tiʔiɬ čxʷəluʔ. 2.40, 2.47	That was all Whale [ever] said.

In other constructions or by itself diɬ is usually glossed by *that, he, she* as in diɬəxʷ *That's it,* or xʷiʔ lədiɬ *He's not the one.*

19.8. Exercises.

I. Below are four sentences and under each are three blank lines labelled (a), (b), and (c). On line (a) write the English gloss of each. On (b) rewrite the original sentence by focusing on the direct complement; and on (c) rewrite the sentence by focusing on the oblique complement. In this exercise any demonstrative may be selected to go before the former predicate.

1. ʔuləkʷᵂtəb ʔə tiʔəʔ pišpiš ti sʔuladxʷ.

    (a) _____.

    (b) _____.

    (c) _____.

2. ʔułiditəb (*tied*) ʔə tiʔəʔ stubš tiʔəʔ X̌əlayʔ (shovel-nose canoe).

    (a) _____.

    (b) _____.

    (c) _____.

3. ʔupusutəb ʔə tiʔił wiwʼsu tiʔəʔ sqʷəbayʔ.

    (a) _____.

    (b) _____.

    (c) _____.

4. ʔučalatəb ʔə tiʔəʔ sqʷəbayʔ tiʔił wiwʼsu.

    (a) _____.

    (b) _____.

    (c) _____.

II. Copy each of the above (b) sentences just created onto a small card or slip of paper -- one sentence per slip -- but in each case omit the oblique complement. Do the same with the (c) sentences but this time omit the direct complement. When this task is completed, shuffle the slips/cards. These are to be used as flash cards. Glance at a card and rapidly express its meaning. Practice until every sentence can be translated without the slightest hesitation.

III.   Translate the following into Lushootseed:

1. What did your mother bring? _____.

2. Who kicked (dᶻubu-d) your dog? _____.

3. Whom did our dog bite? _____.

4. Who kicked you? _____.

5. What did you find? _____.

6. Whom did you help? _____.

7. What scared his dog? _____.

8. Whom did the horse (stiqiw) kick? _____.

LESSON TWENTY

Focus of adjunct and argument

In the preceding lesson the grammar of focused direct and oblique complements was presented. In this lesson the focusing of adjuncts (16.8) and augments (16.6) is treated.

20.1. When the speaker focuses on an adjunct or augment, the predicate is again preceded by a demonstrative as in the cases of focused complements described in Lesson Nineteen. Additionally, the verb of the original predicate (or, if adverbs are present, the first adverb (17.2, 17.2b)) carries either the prefix s- or dəxʷ- * and the appropriate d-paradigm affix (12.4, 12.5). In other words, the original predicate now following a focused adjunct or augment is like the nominalized verb in negatives of existence (18.1, 18.3, 18.6 - 18.6b).

20.2. Of the two prefixes, s- and dəxʷ-, dəxʷ- is the marked member. It indicates the means, place, time, or reason for an event or state in accord with the significance of the focused adjunct or augment. With other concepts s- is used:

    1. qʷɫqʷɫayʔ tiʔiɫ <u>dəxʷ</u>učalads tiʔəʔ sqʷəbayʔ.   With sticks they chased the dog.

    2. sʔuladxʷ tiʔəʔ <u>s</u>uʔəɫəd ʔə tiʔiɫ pišpiš.   A salmon is what the cat ate.

In sentence 1 the focused adjunct, qʷɫqʷɫayʔ *sticks*, expresses the means; therefore, dəxʷ- is said. In number 2, however, the adjunct refers to the patient (because ʔəɫəd is an agent oriented verb (7.4, 7.6)); consequently, s- is the prefix used.

20.2a. Generally, dəxʷ- is replaced by s- when the focused adjunct carries specific grammatical marking for means, place, or time.

    3. q̓čic<u>ab</u> tə <u>s</u>uƛ̓uc̓uds tiʔəʔ sqigʷac.   With a bow he shot this deer.

    4. <u>dxʷʔal</u> tə stuləkʷ tiʔəʔ <u>s</u>uʔibəš ʔə tsiʔiɫ   To the river that old woman walks every
       luƛ ʔal bəkʷ sləxil.   day.

In number 3, the suffix -ab on q̓čic *bow* explicitly conveys the concept *by means of*, therefore, s- replaces dəxʷ-. Similarly, in sentence 4, s- occurs instead of dəxʷ- because dxʷʔal already expresses direction.

20.2b. Sometimes speakers say s- where dəxʷ- would be expected in precise and careful talking. The reverse is never done. In rapid and relaxed speech people sometimes omit the prefix altogether. (In the accompanying texts, omissions of this sort have been amended but always within editorial brackets, e.g., . . . tiʔəʔ [s]uʔəɬəds.)

20.3. Focused adjuncts and augments require d-paradigm affixes (12.4a, 12.5) in the former predicate. The role of these affixes vis a vis verb suffixes is the same as čəd-words. (There is, of course, the added difference that third person (12.4) is specifically marked with a d-paradigm suffix, namely -s, but a corresponding čəd-word is lacking.)

Agent oriented

ʔuʔibəš čəd.	:	. . . dsuʔibəš.	I walked.
ʔuʔibəš.	:	. . . suʔibəšs.	He/she walked.

Patient oriented

ʔupusud čəd.	:	. . . dsupusud.	I threw [something] at [someone].
ʔupusud.	:	. . . supusuds.	He/she threw [something] at [someone].
ʔupusutəb čəd.	:	. . . dsupusutəb.	[Someone] threw [something] at me.
ʔupusutəb.	:	. . . supusutəbs.	[Someone] threw [something] at him/her.

With dəxʷ-, the first person prefix has a special form, namely, d- + dəxʷ- results in cəxʷ-.

ʔupusud čəd	:	. . . dsupusud	:	. . . cəxʷupusud
ʔupusud čəxʷ	:	. . . adsupusud	:	. . . a(d)dəxʷupusud
ʔupusud	:	. . . supusuds	:	. . . dəxʷupusuds
ʔupusud čəɬ	:	. . . supusud čəɬ	:	. . . dəxʷupusud čəɬ
ʔupusud čələp	:	. . . supusudlap	:	. . . dəxʷupusudləp

20.3a. Because **d-paradigm affixes function like čəd-words** (except that the former set has a specific third person marker which the čəd-words lack), they express the agent with agent oriented verbs and also with patient oriented verbs ending in -d (and -dxʷ, -txʷ, -c, and -s) just as čəd-words do. But with patient verbs in -t-əb (and likewise -du-b, -tu-b, -c-əb, and -s-əb) these affixes represent a patient. This, too, is just like čəd-words.

20.3b. The student should pay particular attention to the suffix -s in sentences with focused adjuncts or augments. When a verb of the original predicate is agent oriented, the -s can be replaced by an ʔə-phrase expressing agent.[36] Study the following example set:

5. ʔuʔəɫəd tiʔəʔ pišpiš ʔə ti sʔuladxʷ.   The cat ate the salmon.

5a. sʔuladxʷ tiʔəʔ suʔəɫəd<u>s</u>.   The salmon is what it ate.
    ⤷(agent)

5b. sʔuladxʷ tiʔəʔ suʔəɫəd <u>ʔə tiʔəʔ pišpiš</u>.   The salmon is what the cat ate.

If, however, the verb is patient oriented, the -s represents the patient and, as such, it remains whether or not a direct complement expressing the patient is also present.

6. ʔučalatəb ʔə tiʔiɫ wiw'su ti sqʷəbayʔ ʔə tə qʷɫqʷɫayʔ.   The children chased the dog with sticks.

6a. qʷɫqʷɫayʔ tiʔiɫ dəxʷučalatəb<u>s</u> <u>ti sqʷəbayʔ</u>.   With sticks they chased the dog.
    ⤷(patient)

6b. qʷɫqʷɫayʔ tiʔiɫ dəxʷučalatəb<u>s</u> ʔə tiʔiɫ wiw'su <u>ti sqʷəbayʔ</u>.   With sticks the children chased the dog.
    ⤷ (patient) ⟶

20.4. When interrogative words ask about adjuncts or augments, the resulting questions have the same form as sentences with focused adjuncts and augments; and like these, s-replaces dəxʷ- when the interrogative word or phrase specifically refers to time, place or means. (Compare 20.2a.)

Agent oriented verbs

ʔəsʔəx̌id kʷi <u>dəxʷəstagʷəxʷ</u> <u>ʔə tiʔəʔ qaw'qs</u>.   Why is Raven hungry?

ʔəsčaləxʷ kʷi <u>ɫushuys</u>.   How will he manage?

liɫčad kʷi ɫ(u)<u>adsuʔux̌ʷ</u>.   Which way will you go?

ʔaləxʷ <u>kʷid</u> kʷi sʔukʷ ʔə tsiʔəʔ lux̌.   When is the old woman going home?

---

[36]This ʔə-phrase substitution for -s is the same as that learned for possessive constructions (12.3d).

Patient oriented verbs

ʔəsčal kʷi łuṣhuyudləp tiʔəʔ sʔəłəd čəł.   How will you folks prepare our food?

ṣtab kʷi dəxʷujəctx ʷṣ tiʔił.   What does he use that for?

ṣtab kʷi ṣuhuyyitəbṣ ʔə t(i) adbad tiʔił čaččas.   What is your father making for that boy?
⌣(patient)⌣↗

In this last question, the interrogative ṣtab asks about (i.e., replaces) an adjunct rather than a direct complement because the direct complement has been filled by the yi-role (8.1), tiʔił čaččas. (Review 8.2 through 8.3d.)

20.5. Focusing is an exception to 8.3d. By means of focusing an agent, patient, and yi-role of a single verb can all be expressed in the same sentence even though all three are represented by nouns. (Some would argue that this is possible because the focused item is a clause in its own right and the rest of the sentence including the verb is really a separate but subordinate clause. Clauses are discussed in the next lesson.)

20.6. Dialect differences.

20.6a. In Northern Lushootseed dəxʷ- + lə- (11.3b - 11.6) becomes dəxʷə-. Similarly, s- + lə- becomes sə-. This change does not generally occur in Southern Lushootseed.

20.6b. In Southern Lushootseed sxʷ- (sometimes pronounced as though it were spelled səxʷ-) is said instead of dəxʷ-; and there are no special forms involving the d-paradigm affixes. They are exactly as with s-.

20.6c. Instead of wiwʷsu the Skagit and Sauk-Suiattle say stawigʷał or stawixʷaʔł.

20.7. Exercises.

I. Translate each of the following sentences writing them on a separate sheet of paper. Then close this book and without consulting Lesson Twenty, translate them back into Lushootseed. Open the book and check your work. If any mistakes have been made, look through this lesson (and any other necessary) to find the grammatical point forgotten.

1. čad kʷ(i) adsubəčad ti łapqs (ladle).

2. sʔuladxʷ tiʔəʔ suʔəłəd ʔə ti pišpiš.

3. pišpiš tiʔəʔ ʔuləkʷʷəd ti sʔuladxʷ.

4. čad kʷi subəčads ti x̌ʷubt.

5. čx̌čx̌aʔ (stones) tiʔił supusil ʔə tiʔił wiwˊsu.

6. dił (that is (the place)) tiʔəʔ cəxʷkʷəd(d)xʷ tiʔəʔ dsʔəłəd.

II. Every verb in the sentences below ends in -s, but some of these suffixes are homonyms. On a separate sheet of paper describe the grammatical function of each -s.

1. ʔutəlawis ti sqʷəbayʔ.

2. bəsqʷ tiʔəʔ suʔuləx̌s.

3. qʷˊłayʔ tiʔił dəxʷupusutəbs ti sqʷəbayʔ.

4. ʔułčis tsi sładəyʔ.

5. čx̌aʔ tiʔəʔ dəxʷupusuds ti sqʷəbayʔ.

6. čal kʷi gʷəskʷax̌ʷacids.

LESSON TWENTY-ONE
Clauses

21.1. Consider this sentence from Lesson Fourteen, ɬuxʷakʷʼil čəd ƛuɬ(u)astagʷəxʷəd, *I get tired whenever I am hungry*. A sentence such as this is composed of two smaller sentences called **clauses**. These are ɬuxʷakʷʼil čəd and ƛuɬ(u)astagʷəxʷəd. Without change the first one could serve as an independent sentence. Such clauses are said to be **matrix** or **main** clauses.

The second clause, ƛuɬ(u)astagʷəxʷəd in this case, could not be an independent sentence. It is, therefore, said to be a **subordinate** clause or **embedded sentence**. (The two terms are equivalent.) Of course, one could make a slight change to this second clause, namely replace əd (14.4) with čəd, and it would then be an independent sentence too, but also it would no longer be a part of the original sentence.

21.2. Sentences with subordinate clauses are said to be **complex**. Lushootseed has various types of complex sentences but they are all simply various combinations out of just three basic clause patterns. The student already knows these three patterns but has not yet been given names for them.

21.2a. The most salient feature of each clause pattern is the sort of person marker it has in its predicate (other than person patient suffixes). These three different sets of person markers are listed again here:

I	II	III
čəd	ad/əd	d-/cəxʷ-
čəxʷ	axʷ/əxʷ	ad-
	as/əs	-s
čəɬ	aɬi/əɬi	čəɬ
čələp	aləp/ələp	-ləp

21.2b. Clauses with the first set of person markers are labeled either **čəd-word patterns** or **person particle patterns**. (Reread 17.1a.) Clauses with the second set are called **person clitic patterns**. (Reread 14.1a.) Clauses having the third set of person markers

108

are said to be **nominalized** because, like nouns, they bear the d-paradigm affixes and they require (at least in careful speech) an introductory demonstrative (15.1). They are further characterized by the s- or dəxʷ- prefixes (20.1) although speakers sometimes omit the s- in relaxed speech. (Reread 18.6a and 20.1.).

21.2c. These three clause patterns are contrasted with one another here in the second person singular and third person to refresh the student's memory:

Second person singular

čəd-word pattern	łuʔəłtxʷ čəxʷ ti ʔaciłtalbixʷ.	You will feed the people.
clitic pattern	łuʔəłtxʷəxʷ ti ʔaciłtalbixʷ.	when/if you feed the people.
nominalized pattern	tiʔəʔ ł(u)adsʔəłtxʷ ti ʔaciłtalbixʷ.	what you will feed the people.
čəd-word pattern	łuʔəłtub čəxʷ ʔə ti ʔaciłtalbixʷ.	The people will feed you.
clitic pattern	łuʔəłtubəxʷ ʔə ti ʔaciłtalbixʷ.	when/if the people feed you.
nominalized pattern	tiʔəʔ ł(u)adsʔəłtub ʔə ti ʔaciłtalbixʷ.	what the people will feed you.

Third person

čəd-word pattern	łuʔəłtxʷ ti ʔaciłtalbixʷ.	[Someone] will feed the people.
clitic pattern	łuʔəłtxʷas ti ʔaciłtalbixʷ.	when/if she feeds the people.
nominalized pattern	tiʔəʔ łusəłtxʷs ti ʔaciłtalbixʷ.	what she will feed the people.
čəd-word pattern	łuʔəłtub ʔə ti ʔaciłtalbixʷ.	The people will feed [someone].
clitic pattern	łuʔəłtubəs ʔə ti ʔaciłtalbixʷ.	when/if the people feed him/her.
nominalized pattern	ti łusʔəłtubs ʔə ti ʔaciłtalbixʷ.	what the people will feed him/her.

Students have encountered clitic patterns in Lesson Fourteen and nominalized patterns for focused adjuncts in Lesson Twenty as well as in one type of negative sentence in Lesson Eighteen. In particular, it is a good idea to review thoroughly 20.3a, 20.3b, and 20.4 because statements made there apply to nominalized patterns in general.

21.3. čəd-word patterns are by far the most frequent type in a matrix (main) clause although occasionally a nominalized pattern functions as the matrix clause. čəd-word patterns are also used for one type of relative clause. See 21.6b.

21.4. As presented in Lesson Fourteen, the person clitic pattern is used to form subordinate clauses that are <u>conditional</u>, *if/when*, <u>habitual</u>, *whenever, usually*, or <u>jussive</u>.[37] It is also used following verbs expressing fear. (Reread the model sentences at the end of 14.4.)

21.4a. In conservative Lushootseed style the clitic pattern is also used with interrogative words when these form questions that are embedded in longer sentences. These are exemplified in the (b)-sentences below:

1a. čad kʷi ɫusɫaɫlil čəɫ.	Where are we going to live?
1b. ƛ'abad g̉ʷəčadəs kʷi ɫusɫaɫlil čəɫ.	Guess where we are going to live.
2a. stab kʷi ləg̉ʷəč'əd.	What is he/she looking for?
2b. xʷiʔ kʷi g̉ʷədsəs(h)aydxʷ g̉ʷəstabəs kʷi ləg̉ʷəč'əd.	I don't know what he/she is looking for.
3a. ʔəsčal tiʔəʔ sčətxʷəd.	How is Bear?
3b. ʔuwiliqʷitəb tiʔəʔ sčətxʷəd g̉ʷəsčaləs kʷi x̌əčs.	Bear was asked how his feelings were (i.e., how he felt about things).
4a. g̉ʷat kʷi ɫuc'əlalikʷ.	Who will win?
4b. ʔug̉ʷadadg̉ʷadəxʷ əlg̉ʷəʔ g̉ʷəg̉ʷatəs kʷi ɫuc'əlalikʷ.	They discussed who would win.
5a. pə(d)tab kʷi ɫusɫčils.	When will he/she get here?
5b. ʔəxʷcutəb čəxʷ ʔu g̉ʷəpə(d)tabəs kʷi g̉ʷəsɫčils.	Do you think he/she will get here sometime?

---

[37]Jussive clauses are those that follow commands, orders, requests, and the like.

6a. kʷidid kʷi diʔaʔ.   How many people are here?

6b. xʷiʔ kʷi gʷədsəslax̌dxʷ gʷə́kʷʷididəs   I don't remember how many people
    kʷi diʔaʔ.   are here.

If what follows the embedded interrogative is another subordinate clause (as in these (b)-sentences), it will be nominalized or not according to 19.5 and 20.4. (Contrast 2a/2b with 5a/5b.)

21.4b. In less conservative styles, speakers very often omit the special clitic marking from embedded interrogative words. For example, in a story from the second volume of this reader there is the following sentence:

xʷiʔəxʷ [kʷi] gʷəsəs(h)aydxʷs <u>ʔəsčal</u>   [He] did not know how he was going
kʷi łudəxʷhuydxʷs.   to manage to do it.

The third person clitic {as/əs} is missing from ʔəsčal (as well as the usual subjunctive prefix {gʷ-}).

21.5. Nominalized subordinate clauses are far more frequently encountered than the clitic type. The student is already familiar with the nominalized pattern in one kind of negation (18.6, 18.6a) and with focused adjuncts and augments (20.1). Also they fill three of the constituents (sentences parts) presented in **Lesson Sixteen**, namely, the direct complement, adjunct and augment. (The examples that follow all come from the four stories of this reader's first volume.)

21.5a. Nominalized subordinate clauses can serve as direct complements to predicates with patient oriented verbs:

ʔulax̌dxʷəxʷ <u>tiʔił tushuy ʔə tiʔił c̓ix̌c̓ix̌.</u>   [He] remembered what Fish Hawk had done.

ʔušudxʷ <u>tiʔił səsqʷʷuʔ ʔə tiʔił ʔiišəds ʔal tiʔəʔ</u>   [He] saw his friends gathered
<u>hikʷ č̓x̌aʔ.</u>   around this big boulder.

x̌ʷul' čəd łuləʔux̌ʷtxʷ <u>tiʔəʔ ł(u)adsʔəłtxʷ.</u>   I will just take [to them] what you are [planning] to feed [them].

ʔəs(h)aydxʷ <u>tiʔił x̌useʔibəš ʔə tiʔił dukʷibəł.</u>   [He] knew that Changer would be traveling.

ɬuhuyutəbəxʷ čʼit <u>tiʔiɬ dəxʷʔibəš čəɬ</u>.

[It] will make near where we travel (i.e., it will shorten the distance we have to walk).

21.5b. Nominalized subordinate clauses can serve as adjuncts. Sometimes these adjuncts convey the patient of an agent oriented verb as in the first example below. Often they are adjuncts expressing time, place, manner and the like.

yəcəbaxʷ ti luχ <u>ʔə tiʔiɬ sɬaliltubsəxʷ</u>.

The old man told [the villagers] about [someone's] being brought ashore.

ʔəsx̌icil tiʔiɬ čʼχaʔ <u>ʔə tiʔiɬ sučalads tiʔiɬ sbiaw</u>.

Boulder was angry as he chased Coyote.

x̌ʷulʼ ləcuʔiʔɬadəb ʔə tiʔəʔ <u>ʔə tiʔiɬ χʼusqʷʼəls</u>.

All [he was doing was] eating the berries [off the bushes] as they ripened.

hikʷ ləcutukʷʼucut <u>ʔə tiʔiɬ sətəčs, ʔə tiʔiɬ sčalads tiʔiɬ sbiaw</u>.

[It] made a great thumping sound as it rolled, as it chased Coyote.

21.5c. Many of these subordinate clauses are augments that explain the motivation for the act or the reason for the state conveyed in the main clause.

χʼuʔahild əlgʷəʔ <u>ɬudəxʷʔa(h)s kʷi stab ɬusʔəɬəds əlgʷəʔ</u>.[38]

They would put it [away] so there would be something for them to eat.

ləcuʔabyid čəɬ tiʔəʔ čʼχaʔ ʔə tiʔəʔ stabigʷs čəɬ <u>tiʔəʔ ɬusʔibəš čəɬ</u>.

We are giving our belongings to this boulder because we are going on a trip.

diɬ[39] <u>dəxʷutʼasad čəɬ tiʔəʔ čʼχaʔ</u>.

That is why we pay this boulder.

---

[38]The final part of the nominalized subordinate clause, namely, ɬusʔəɬəds əlgʷəʔ, is itself another subordinate clause which modifies (i.e., goes with) stab. See 21.6a.

[39]After diɬ speakers very often omit the demostrative normally expected to introduce a following noun or nominalized subordinate clause.

diɬ <u>daỷ X̌uscut ʔə tiʔiɬ sč̓ətx̌ʷəd.</u>

ɬuʔa(h) čəxʷ [tiʔiɬ] x̌ʷul' ɬ(u)adsyubil.

That is all Bear would say.

You will be there until you starve [to death].

21.6. Sometimes a subordinate clause modifies (i.e., goes with/belongs to) a particular noun. Clauses that modify a noun are called **relative clauses**. In Lushootseed relative clauses have either the čəd-word pattern or the nominalized pattern except that these nominal clauses are not introduced by a demonstrative.

21.6a. If the relationship between that noun and the verb of the modifying clause is like that of adjuncts, then the relative clause has the nominalized pattern (except for the absence of an 'introductory' demonstrative).

bəčatəbəxʷ tiʔiɬ kʷat'aq <u>dəxʷʔibəš ʔə tiʔiɬ bibščəb ʔi tiʔiɬ suʔsuqʷaʔs.</u>

Wall-lining mats were laid down for Little Mink and his little younger brother to walk on.

ʔuqʷuʔəd tiʔiɬ stab <u>gʷədəxʷ(h)əliʔis(s) əlgʷəʔ.</u>

[They] gathered things they could live on.

X̌uʔahild əlgʷəʔ tiʔiɬ ɬudəxʷʔa(h)s kʷi stab <u>ɬus[u]ʔəɬəds əlgʷəʔ.</u>

They would put it [away] so something would be there for them to eat.

ʔupačad tiʔiɬ stabigʷs <u>sʔabyids.</u>

He displayed the goods he was giving [to Boulder].

21.6b. When the relationship between the noun and the verb of the modifying clause is not like that of adjuncts, then the relative clause has the čəd-word pattern. (Note that nothing distinguishes these clauses from independent main clauses except the speaker's vocal flow. If the speaker makes what might be called a 'period pause' between the two clauses, then each is a main clause independent of the other. If, however, they are pronounced as a single flowing sentence, the second clause is considered to be a relative modifying the final noun of the first clause.)

ʔəs(h)aydxʷ čəd tsi sɬadəỷ <u>ʔəsɬaɬlil ʔal tiʔiɬ.</u>

I know the woman who lives there.

ʔəs(h)aydxʷ čəd tsi sɬadəỷ.

+

ʔəsɬaɬlil ʔal tiʔiɬ.

I know the woman.

+

She lives there.

ʔušudxʷ čəd ti sqʷəbayʔ <u>ʔudᶻubutəb ʔə tiʔiɫ čʼačʼas</u>.	I saw the dog that boy kicked.
ʔušudxʷ čəd ti sqʷəbayʔ.	I saw the dog.
+	+
ʔudᶻubutəb ʔə tiʔiɫ čʼačʼas.	That boy kicked [it].
ʔušudxʷ čəxʷ ʔu ti čʼačʼas <u>ʔudᶻubud tiʔiɫ sqʷəbayʔ</u>.	Did you see the boy who kicked that dog?
ʔušudxʷ čəxʷ ʔu ti čʼačʼas.	Did you see the boy?
+	+
ʔudᶻubud tiʔiɫ sqʷəbayʔ.	[He] kicked that dog.

21.6c. When relative clauses of the čəd-word pattern are short, they can precede rather than follow the nouns they modify. (The first three examples in 17.4b provide examples.)

21.7. Some sentences have two or even more main clauses. These are said to be **compound** (or **coordinate**) sentences. When first or second persons are involved, the čəd-words have a special joining form which consists of the addition of a final a-vowel.

čəda *and I*   čxʷa *and you*   čɫa *and we*   čələpa *and you folks*

21.7a. Just as čəd-words follow the first word in their clause be it a verb, adverb (17.3, 17.3b), or some other type of predicate word (16.1), so too these compound čəd-words follow the first constituent (16.4) in their sentence, namely, the first clause.

ƛub čəɫ ʔuhudčup <u>čɫa</u> ʔukʷukʷcut.	We should make a fire <u>and we</u> [should] cook.
dayʼ čəxʷ ɫuʔəƛʼ dxʷʔal tiʔiɫ dʼalʔal <u>čəda</u> ɫuʔəɫtubicid.	After a while you will come to my house <u>and I</u> will feed you.
hiwiləxʷ <u>čxʷa</u> tqad tə šəgʷɫ.	Go ahead <u>and (you)</u> close the door.

21.7b. Compound sentences involving third person have no special marking. Only the speaker's voice can distinguish a compound from two separate sentences. On the printed page one may write a comma to separate one main clause of a compound from the other.

21.7. Exercises.

I. In 21.4 four meanings expressed with the clitic pattern subordinate clause are listed. On a separate sheet of paper copy out the ten example sentences at the very end of 14.4 and label each by its meaning according to 21.4, e.g., *conditional*, *habitual*, etc.

II. Each of the six sentences below has at least one subordinate clause of the nominative pattern. Underline the subordinate clause or clauses in each and in the margin to the left write the paragraph number from the lesson that accounts for (or describes the reason for) each subordinate clause.

___ 1. ʔukʷəd(d)xʷ tiʔił supusutəbs tiʔəʔ wiwˀsu.

He managed to catch what was thrown at the children.

___ 2. dił tiʔə cəxʷkʷəd(d)xʷ tiʔəʔ dsʔəłəd.

That is where I got my food.

___ 3. dᶻux̌ʷatəxʷ ʔə tiʔəʔ p̓q̓ac tusuʔəłəds.

He vomited this rotten wood he'd been eating.

___ 4. x̌ʷulʼ čəxʷ ləʔux̌ʷ dxʷʔal kʷ(i) adsłčil.

You just keep going until you arrive.

___ 5. ʔukʷədad tiʔəʔ qʷuʔ dəxʷucʼagʷači(ʔ)b ʔal tiʔəʔ sbałs.

He took some water he uses to wash his with hands when he cures.

___ 6. x̌ʷulʼ čəd łuləʔux̌ʷtxʷ tiʔəʔ ł(u)adsʔəłtxʷ əlgʷəʔ.

I'll just take [i.e., deliver to them] what you are going to feed them.

III. Study the following sentence and its gloss. Then answer the questions below.

xʷiʔəxʷ gʷəsəs(h)aydxʷs [gʷ]əsčal[əs] kʷi łudəxʷhuydxʷs kʷi gʷədəxʷləkʷˀdxʷs tiʔił sʔəłəd ʔə tiʔəʔ ʔalšs. *He didn't know how he was going to manage to eat his sister's food.*

How many clauses (of all kinds) are there in this sentence? _____.

Copy the matrix (main) clause onto this blank. _____.

Among the subordinate clauses in this sentence how many have the clitic pattern? _.

The English gloss *he is going to manage* corresponds to what Lushootseed in the above sentence?

_____.

How would one write the Lushootseed equivalent for, *You will manage to eat my salmon?*

_____.

LESSON TWENTY-TWO

Some final points on grammar

In the preceding twenty-one lessons the major grammatical features of Lushootseed have been presented. There remain only a few points to be considered before the student is ready to read the language. Of the items considered immediately below, only 22.1b, 22.4, and 22.8 are required for reading the four texts of this reader.

22.1. More patient suffixes:

22.1a. A few frequently heard verb stems have -š instead of -d (page 10):

ʔabš	give something
ʔišłš	paddle it (a canoe)
łalš	take something off/out of the fire
ƛ̓alš	put it on (an article of clothing), wear it
suxʷtəš	recognize someone/something
tagʷš	buy something
təbaš	crave something

22.1b. A few other stems permit either -d or -š:

bəčaš / bəčad	set someone/something down
dəgʷaš / dəgʷad	put something inside a container
łaq̓aš / łaq̓ad	set someone/someting down
ƛ̓agʷš / ƛ̓agʷad	stitch (i.e., make) a mat
p̓t̓aš / p̓t̓ad	put something away, save it; tidy up an area
qʷataš / qʷatad	lay something down
t̓agʷtəš / t̓agʷtəd	put something on top of something
x̌alš / x̌alad	write something down, mark something

(The fourth set, ƛ̓agʷš / ƛ̓agʷad, and the last, x̌alš / x̌alad, are unusual in having a vowel before -d but not before -š.)

116

There is some variation among speakers concerning the use of these endings. In Northern Lushootseed, speakers of Snohomish use -š a little less often than others.

22.1c. All the words in the second group (22.1b) take the ending sequence -t-əb (6.1) whether they otherwise end in -š or -d. Members of the first set, however, are more irregular. Instead of -t-əb, the forms ƛal(š) and tagʷ(š) have -ib:

ʔuƛ'al<u>ib</u> ʔə tiʔiɫ stubš ti šiqʷ.   The man put the hat on.

ʔutagʷ<u>ib</u> ʔə ti dʔalš tiʔiɫ puʔtəd.   My brother bought that shirt.

On the other hand, neither ʔišɫ nor suxʷt- permit either -t-əb or -ib although ʔišɫ can have -tu-b as in ʔuʔišɫtub *[Someone] tried out [a canoe] (to see how it handled).* The texts lack information on this point concerning təbaš.

22.2. A few conservative speakers replace -t-əb with -t-id when the verb is in a subordinate clause formed with the nominalized pattern (21.2b).

x̌ʷul' ƛ(u)aswačbid tiʔiɫ ƛ(u)ashuyu<u>tid</u> tiʔəʔ sləxil.   He was just watching what was done with the daylight.

diʔɫ[40] kʷi skʷədat<u>id</u> ʔə tiʔəʔ p'əč'əb tiʔəʔ sqqʷus.   Unexpectedly Bobcat took a small canoe mat.

ʔəsdukʷtxʷ tiʔəʔ ʔiišəds ʔə tiʔəʔ sələkʷ<u>ti[d]</u> tiʔəʔ sxʷiʔxʷiʔs.   He was angry with his people in that they were his game.

Very often this suffix, -tid, is pronounced without the final d, either as -tiʔ or simply -ti. (Comparing Lushootseed to other Salish languages suggests that in former times -tid was the usual form in these subordinate clauses. Today, however, it is little heard although more so among the Skagit than elsewhere.)

22.3. The suffix -agʷid no longer occurs in Lushootseed speech, but it has been preserved on tape recordings made in the early 1950's of people conversing and telling stories -- people who then were in their nineties and older. This suffix was added to truncated forms of -du-, -tu-, and to the -t- of -d/-t- (and presumably to -s- and -c-)[41] to indicate the

---

[40]See 22.9 below.

[41]Note the similarity in form between this suffix and the reciprocal suffix (9.6b). This similarity results from the fact that both suffixes share the element -agʷ- which was at one

speaker's chief topic of interest even though the grammar placed that topic in a subordinate role.

The following example helps elucidate the significance of -agʷid. It occurs in line 5 below:

1. ʔukʷədatəb ʔə tiʔəʔ pʼəčʼəb.   Bobcat took it.

2. ʔukʷədad tiʔəʔ pʼəčʼəbulicʼaʔs.   [He] took his bobcat-blanket.

3. gʷəl ʔald kʷədiʔ ʔadzalus ...   And [he] put it in a beautiful ... [place]...

4. gʷəl ləgʷədil ʔəxʷčəgʷus.   And he sat facing the water.

5. diʔɬ kʷi (s)šudəgʷi[d] ʔə tiʔəʔ čačʼas. All of a sudden the child saw him.

6. 'diɬəxʷ bayəʔ!   'That's Daddy!

7. diɬəxʷ bayəʔ!'   That's Daddy!'

8. diɬ ti pʼəčʼəb ti ʔucut(t)əb ʔə   It was Bobcat whom the noble child spoke
   tiʔəʔ sqaqagʷəɬ.   of.

In the first four lines Bobcat clearly is the topic of discourse and he is the agent. Line 5, however, introduces a new agent, the child; but by using the suffix -agʷid (here pronounced as -əgʷi), the speaker is in effect saying to the addressee, "I've introduced a new agent now but my primary interest remains with Bobcat." Line 8 proves that the story teller's attention has remained with Bobcat.[42]

22.4. Nouns in direct relation with verbs meaning *become* and *make* typically lack a modifying demonstrative (15.1). Here follow a few examples:

ʔuhuyiləxʷ bəščəb.   He has become a mink.

ʔuhuyil čəd kiaʔ ʔal ti dukʷəɬdat.   I became a grandmother yesterday.

... ʔal kʷi tusəshuys əlgʷəʔ tuʔaciɬtalbixʷ.   ... when they were made people.

ʔuhuyud čəd xʷubt.   I made a paddle [out of it].

---

time a full suffix in its own right.

[42]Students are encouraged to read a particularly lucid description of this suffix (and its related forms in other Salish languages) in M. Dale Kinkade. 1990. Sorting out Third Persons in Salishan Discourse, *International Journal of American Linguistics*, 56: 341-360.

In the above examples all verbs are based on the root huy. The same absence of determiners obtains in constructions with other verbs meaning *make* such as šəɫ / čəɫ discussed in the next section. (The Swinomish and Skagit say čəɫ instead of šəɫ.)

22.5. Compounding is relatively rare in Lushootseed. Nevertheless, there is a special productive subtype that the student will encounter occasionally. It is called **noun incorporation**. Contrast these two sentences:

    1. ʔutag^wš tə <u>səpləl</u>.   [Someone] bought some bread.

    2. ʔutəx^wsəpləl.   [Someone] bought bread.

Both tag^w- (22.1a) and təx^w mean *buy*, but the second verb cannot take a patient suffix such as -d, -š, or any other. Without a patient suffix the verb would not be expected to have a patient noun. Instead, that noun joins with the verb stem creating a new stem of the type verb + noun. The noun is said to be incorporated into the verb. This new stem is agent oriented.

    2a. ʔu<u>təx^wsəpləl</u> tsi dʔalš.   My sister bought bread.

Noun incorporation provides Lushootseed speakers with still another way of expressing both an agent and patient in one clause. Of course, speakers can also convey both roles in the more usual way as in 1a below:

    1a. ʔu<u>tag^w</u>ib ʔə tsi dʔalš tə səpləl.   My sister bought some bread.

22.5a. Typically speakers elect to use the incorporated formation when the activity occurs so regularly that the patient is only barely noteworthy. Thus, in 2 and 2a the speaker is letting us know that this bread buying is an absolutely ordinary event, while sentences 1 and 1a are pointing out that bread is the matter of concern.

    We see, then, that Lushootseed grammar provides speakers with a scale of focus:

ʔutəx^wsəpləl tsi dʔalš.   My sister bought bread.

ʔutag^wib ʔə tsi dʔalš tə səpələl.   My sister bought some bread.

səpləl ti ʔutag^wib ʔə tsi dʔalš.   Bread is what my sister bought.

Reread the introduction to Lesson Nineteen.

22.5b. As pointed out above, verb stems that can be a part of these noun incorporations do not take patient suffixes. However, the incorporated stem can do so. Consider the following sentence wherein the noun ƛ̓əbiɫəd *rope* is added to the verb šəɫ *make*:

diɫ tiʔəʔ dəxʷšəɬt'əbiɬədtubs.   It was used for making rope.

Here the patient suffix sequence -tu-b (6.1) has been added to the verb + noun stem. (The prefix dəxʷ- (20.2) is glossed as *used for*. The final suffix -s is triggered by dəxʷ-(20.1).)

22.5c . A third verb that incorporates nouns is λ̓a *go*. It is equivalent to ʔuxʷ dxʷʔal. Compare the following:

ləλ̓atawd čəd.   = ləʔuxʷ čəd dxʷʔal (ti) tawd.   I'm on my way to town.

22.5d. Verbs that ordinarily take patient suffixes can be converted to verbs requiring noun incorporation by means of the suffix -əɬ-.   For example, one can say ʔučaləɬpišpiš ti sq̓ʷəbayʔ instead of ʔučalatəb ʔə ti sq̓ʷəbayʔ ti pišpiš. Both mean that *the dog chased the cat*, but the first implies that the agent is acting with his/her own interests paramount.

22.5e. The cohesion between verb and noun in these incorporated constructions is not always as 'tight' as the above examples imply because čəd-words can optionally occur between verb and noun when there is no patient suffix.   The same is true of the other predicate particles (17.1a).   Compare the following sentence pairs:

ʔušəɬt'əbiɬəd čəd.	= ʔušəɬ čəd t'əbiɬəd.	I made rope.
ʔutəxʷsəpləl čəd.	= ʔutəxʷ čəd səpləl.	I bought bread.
ʔušəɬxʷʔax̌ʷaʔəd ʔu.	= ʔušəɬ ʔu xʷʔax̌ʷaʔəd.	Did [she] make a clam basket?
ʔuλ̓a tawd čəɬ.	= ʔuλ̓a čəɬ tawd.	We went to town.

Similarly, the clitic axʷ (14.2 - 14.3b) occasionally separates the incorporated element from the verb as seen in this sentence, cutəxʷ ti tuɬʔal tiʔiɬ diʔucid da̱ʔəɬəxʷ Vancouver, *These from that [place] across the water named now Vancouver spoke now.*

Nevertheless, a demonstrative (otherwise obligatory before the noun) is not possible in the sentences on the right.   This absence establishes the unity between these verbs and nouns as being morphological (i.e., wordbuilding) rather than just syntactic.

22.6. Just as λ̓a *go* (22.5c) can be thought of as including dxʷʔal *to, toward* in its meaning, so too, ɬil *give food/drink to someone* can be thought of as including -yi- (8.1).

ʔuɬild tsi luλ̓.   [Someone] gave [some food] to the old woman.

ʔuɬild ʔə ti λ̓xʷayʔ.   [Someone] gave a dog salmon [to someone].

ʔuɬiltəb ʔə ti stubš.   The man gave [some food to someone].

ʔutiltəb tsiʔəʔ čəgʷas(s) ʔə tiʔəʔ səsqʷəls. — [They] gave his wife their roasted (food).

ʔutiltəb čəd ʔə tiʔəʔ qa(h) — I was given one full backpack [of elk meat]

dəčʼuʔ sčəbaʔ tiʔəʔ dsčəbaʔtub, cəxʷutiltəb. — which was put on my back, when I was given food.

22.6a. A similar construction can be formed with the stem həliʔ whose ultimate meaning signifies *live, alive, life, soul.*

tugʷəx̌alijəd čət tiʔəʔ ds(h)əliʔdub ʔə ti sʔubʔubədiʔ. — We will unwrap this [elk meat] given to me by the hunters.

ʔu· siʔab, tux̌ʷ čələp tuhəliʔdxʷəxʷ kʼi dbədbədaʔ. — Oh, sirs! You save my children [by your gift].

The idea is that the recipient is able to survive only because of the gift of food or drink. In fact, the expression for *thank you*, appropriate only for a gift or food or beverage, is həliʔdubš čəxʷ, literally, *You save me.*

22.7. By means of the word sgʷaʔ *one's own* the concept of ownership can be emphasized. The d-paradigm affixes are used with it.

ti dsgʷaʔ. — It's mine.

ckʷaqid t(u)adsgʷaʔ. — It will always be yours.

dit tə hikʷ ʔalʔal tə sgʷaʔ čət. — The big house is ours.

xʷiʔ lədsgʷaʔ dsqʷəbayʔ. — It's not my dog.

dit dsgʷaʔ dpišpiš. — That is my very own cat.

When there is a sequence of sgʷaʔ plus a noun expressing the item possessed as in the last two examples above, speakers optionally omit the d-paradigm affix from the noun expressing the item owned: dit dsgʷaʔ pišpiš.

22.8. Many sentences, especially in long narratives, begin with one of or a combination of a small set of words called **sentential adverbs**. The most common are gʷəl *and, but, or,* huy *then, next,* and hay *next.* The difference in meaning between the last two is subtle and difficult to gloss in English. A common variant of gʷəl is gʷaʔ.

22.8a. Often they are said in various combinations such as gʷəl (h)uy, hay gʷəl, huy gʷəl all more or less meaning *and then.* Some speakers frequently use ʔah *located, (be) there* for the same purpose either singly or in combination with one of the sentential adverbs.

22.8b. The sentential adverb gʷəl is also used to **topicalize.** Topicalization is achieved by placing gʷəl after the topic, in affect treating the topic as an entire clause and using gʷəl to introduce the following clause. Below is a short description of some clams. The first and fourth sentences are topicalized, but in the second and third, gʷəl is simply linking one sentence to another:

1. haʔəc gʷəl həlaʔb hikʷ sʔax̌ʷuʔ.	As for the horse clam, it is a really big clam.
2. gʷəl ʔəspʼil tiʔəʔ čawəyʼs.	And its shell is flat.
3. gʷəl tux̌ʷ (h)uy ʔəsbulux̌ʷ tiʔəʔ čawəyʼ ʔə tsiʔəʔ sx̌əpʼab.	But in contrast the shell of the cockle is round.
4. gʷəl tiʔəʔ sʔax̌ʷuʔ gʷəl ʔudəgʷabacbid ʔə tiʔəʔ saliʔ.	And as for the butter clam, it is between the [other] two.

In the fourth sentence, the first gʷəl is just linking this sentence to the preceding ones. It is the second gʷəl that topicalizes tiʔəʔ sʔax̌ʷuʔ *this butter clam.* In the third sentence the sentential adverb combination gʷəl (h)uy has been separated by the predicate adverb (17.2) tux̌ʷ *in contrast.*

22.9. Finally, the student's attention is directed to the two words dił and diʔł. They occur over and over in Lushootseed discourse. In spite of their similar pronunciations, they have very different meanings. The former, dił (19.4, 19.7), *the one(s) who, that which, the one referred to,* is a pronoun. The second one, diʔł, means *suddenly, all at once, abruptly; might.* Both of these words are used most often as one word predicates which are followed by a subordinate clause of the s-/dəxʷ- types (21.5).

UNIT FOUR

ANSWERS

ANSWERS TO GRAMMAR QUESTIONS

Lesson One, pages 3, 4:   Where does the **verb** (the action word) come in a Lushootseed sentence -- first or last? <u>First</u>. What does ti čʼačʼas mean? <u>The boy</u>. In sentences numbered 1, 4, and 6 does ti čʼačʼas perform the action; that is, in 1, 4, and 6 is ti čʼačʼas the **agent** (the doer)? <u>Yes</u>. Is ti čʼačʼas the agent in sentences 2, 3, and 5 or is it the **patient** (the one to whom some act is done)? <u>Patient</u>. On the following blank write what it is in these Lushootseed sentences that tells the reader or listener whether ti čʼačʼas is agent or patient. <u>If the verb ends in -txʷ, ti čʼačʼas is patient</u>. What does ʔutʼukʷ mean? <u>Go home</u>.

Lesson Two, page 6: What does čəd mean? <u>I</u>. What does čəɫ mean? <u>We</u>. Do these two words express the agent or the patient in their sentences? <u>Agent</u>. I went home. = ʔutʼukʷ čəd. We brought the boy. = ʔuʔəƛʼtxʷ čəɫ ti čʼačʼas. I took the boy home. = ʔutʼukʷtxʷ čəd ti čʼačʼas.

Lesson Two, page 7: What does the little word ʔu mean? <u>Question</u>. (Such little words are called **particles** by linguists.) Where in the sentence does it occur? <u>Right after čəxʷ or čələp. If there is no čəxʷ nor čələp, it goes right after the verb</u>. What is the difference in meaning between čəxʷ and čələp? <u>The first is *you singular* while the latter is *you plural, you folks*</u>. . . . Cross out the inappropriate English word: <u>čələp = ye, čəxʷ = thou</u>.

Lesson Three, page 9, (3.1): What is the difference in meaning between ti čʼačʼas (in Lessons One and Two) and tsi čʼačʼas (of this lesson)? <u>Gender (i.e., male and female)</u>. . . . Write the English meanings beside each . . . . sʔuladxʷ = <u>salmon</u>, čʼačʼas = <u>child</u>, sqʷəbayʔ = <u>dog</u>.

Lesson Three, page 10, (3.2): Three new sets of verbs occur in this lesson. Note their **suffixes** (endings). Does an agent or patient follow the suffix -d? <u>Patient</u>. In this respect is -txʷ like -d or -b? <u>-d</u>. In Lesson One there are three verbs that have no suffixes at all. Does the following noun (when expressed) represent the agent or the patient? <u>Agent</u>. In this respect are the suffixless verbs in Lessons One and Two like those ending in -d or those ending in -b? <u>-b</u>.

125

Lesson Four, page 13: Do the nouns in these (a)-sentences express agents or patients? Agents. All verbs in the (a)-sentences end in what suffix? -il . For similarity in grammatical function should this suffix be matched with -b or with -txʷ and -d? -b. Do the nouns in the (b)-sentences convey agents or patients? Patients. All verbs in the (b)-sentences end in what suffix? -is. For similarity in grammatical functions, should this suffix be matched with -b or with -txʷ and -d? With -txʷ and -d.

Lesson Four, page 14: List the four verbs from the (a)-sentences 1 through 4 above in one column and those from this second set of (a)-sentences, 5 through 8, in an adjacent column. Beside each verb write its gloss.

1 through 4	English glosses	5 through 8	English glosses
ʔuʔusil	dove	ʔuxʷit'il	fell off
ʔutəlawil	ran	ʔucɬil	bled
ʔuɬalil	went ashore	ʔuƛ̓uxʷil	got cold
ʔuɬčil	arrived	ʔuččil	became red

Lesson Six, page 22: Each (a)-sentence has how many nouns? One. How many nouns are there in each (b)-sentence? One. In the (c)-sentences, does the first noun following the particle ʔə stand for an agent or a patient? Agent . What does the other noun in the (c)-sentences represent? Patient. What suffix do all verbs in the (c)-sentences share that is lacking in all the (b)-sentences? -(ə)b. What seems to be the function (purpose) of this new suffix? It provides for an agent noun with a patient oriented verb.

Lesson Six, page 24: What is the function (purpose) of ʔə in these sentences? It distinguishes the agent from the patient by specifically tagging the agent. Without ʔə would it always be possible to distinguish agent from patient? No.

Following the sequence patient suffix + -b, do čəd-words express the agent or the patient? Patient. Where does the interrogative particle, ʔu, occur in the sentence relative to the čəd-words? It follows the čəd-words. Where does it occur relative to the particle ʔə? It is before the particle ʔə.

Lesson Eight, page 34: Describe how the role (function) of ti č̓ač̓as in sentence 2 differs from the role of ti č̓ač̓as in sentence 3. In 2 ti č̓ač̓as is beneficiary while in 3 it is patient. Is the role of ti č̓ač̓as in sentence 2 approximately the same as in sentence 4 or are their functions entirely different? <u>Same</u>. What is the name of the role of ti čačas in sentence 1? <u>Agent</u>. What is the name of the role of ti čačas in sentence 3? <u>Patient</u>.

Lesson Eight, page 35 (8.2a,b): In sentences with -yi- how are patient and -yi-role distinguished? <u>The patient is tagged with the particle ʔə</u>. How are patient and agent distinguished in sentences with -yi-? <u>By word order. The agent is first in the sentence</u>.

Lesson Eight, page 36 (8.3a,b,c): What are the roles of the two nouns in sentence 9 and in which order do they occur? <u>They are agent and patient and occur in that order</u>. What are the roles and relative order of the two nouns in sentence 10? <u>They are agent and yi-role in that order</u>. What are the roles and relative order of the two nouns in sentence 11? <u>These are yi-role and patient in that order</u>.

Lesson Ten, pages 45-46: Contrast 1a with 1b and 2a with 2b. The first word in each pair of sentences is identical except for what? <u>ʔu- versus ʔəs-</u>. Now add to this list the words having the ʔəs- prefix from the sentences at the beginning of this lesson numbered 1b through 4b writing them in the blanks on the left.

<u>ʔəsqʼaxʷ</u>	<u>frozen</u>
<u>ʔəsʔitut</u>	<u>asleep</u>
<u>ʔəsɬid</u>	<u>tied</u>
<u>ʔəsɬačʼ</u>	<u>extinguished</u>

Lesson Twelve, page 59: Translate the sentences below into Lushootseed:

We looked for Mary's dog.	<u>ʔugʷəčʼəd čəɬ ti sqʷəbayʔ ʔə tsi mali.</u> or <u>ʔugʷəčʼəb čəɬ ʔə ti sqʷəbayʔ ʔə tsi mali.</u>
It ate the old woman's salmon.	<u>ʔuləkʷʷəd ti sʔuladxʷ ʔə tsi luX</u> or <u>ʔuʔəɬəd ʔə ti sʔuladxʷ ʔə tsi luX.</u>
She roasted the boy's salmon.	<u>ʔuqʷʷəld ti sʔuladxʷ ʔə ti čačas.</u> or <u>ʔuqʷʷəlb ʔə ti sʔuladxʷ ʔə ti čačas.</u>
He took the old man's paddle.	<u>ʔukʷədad ti XʷubT ʔə ti luX.</u>

(12.4). Compare the following words with one another and with those listed in 12.3d above. Provide the missing English gloss on each blank.

dx̌ʷubt	my paddle	x̌ʷubt čəɬ	our paddle
dsqʷəbayʔ	my dog	sqʷəbayʔ čəɬ	our dog
dšawʼ	my bone	šawʼ čəɬ	our bone
adx̌ʷubt	your paddle	x̌ʷubtləp	(the) paddle of you folks
adsqʷəbayʔ	your dog	sqʷəbayʔləp	(the) dog of you folks
adšawʼ	your bone	šawʼləp	(the) bone of you folks

Lesson Fourteen, page 70: Aside from the vowel difference (because clitics are sometimes stressed (14.2a) but čəd-words never are), the student should find a total of three differences between the above two lists. Two of these differences are specific to this or that particular person marker. The other difference separates one entire set from the other. On the lines below students should describe each difference.

1. The clitic set lacks the initial č-.
2. There is a third person form, namely, -as/-əs in the clitic set.
3. In the first person plural the clitic set has a final i-vowel lacking in the čəd-word set.

Lesson Fourteen, pages 72-73 (14.7c): The derivational suffix -šad occurs in two different stems in the example sentences of 14.4b. Write both stems here: -čʼəlpšad- and -x̌ʷəƛ̕šad. What two glosses are given for -šad? ankle and leg. Specifically, -šad designates the *foot* **and** the *leg* (especially from *below the knee*).

Lesson Eighteen, page 95: With the word čʼəx̌bidac *yew tree* create the following sentences: 1. That is not a yew tree. x̌ʷiʔ ləčʼəx̌bidac tiʔiɬ. 2. There are no yew trees around here. x̌ʷiʔ kʷi gʷəcʼəx̌bidac ʔal tiʔaʔ. 3. We do not have [any] yew trees. x̌ʷiʔ kʷi gʷəcʼəx̌bidac čəɬ.

Lesson Eighteen, page 97 (18.7): The suffix -txʷ bound to the negative adverb, x̌ʷiʔ, is the same suffix encountered in Lesson One, the causative. How would one say in Lushootseed, *Don't let me cry*? x̌ʷiʔtubš ləx̌aab.

ANSWERS TO EXERCISES

Lesson One

1. ʔuʔux̌ʷ. 2. ʔuťukʷtxʷ ti čačas. 3. ʔuʔəƛ’txʷ ti čačas. 4. ʔuʔəƛ’txʷ.
5. ʔuʔux̌ʷtxʷ. 6. ʔuʔəƛ’. 7. ʔuťukʷ. 8. ʔuťukʷtxʷ. 9. ʔuʔəƛ’ ti čačas. 10. ʔuʔux̌ʷ
ti čačas. 11. ʔuťukʷtxʷ ti čačas. 12. ʔuťukʷ ti čačas.

Lesson Two

1. ʔuʔux̌ʷ. 2. ʔuʔəƛ’txʷ čəd ti čačas. 3. ʔuʔəƛ’ čəɬ. 4. ʔuťukʷtxʷ čələp ʔu ti
čačas. 5. ʔuťukʷtxʷ čələp ʔu. 6. ʔuťukʷtxʷ ʔu ti čačas. 7. ʔuʔux̌ʷtxʷ čəxʷ ʔu.
8. ʔuťukʷtxʷ čəxʷ ʔu.

Lesson Three

1. ʔuqʷʷəld čələp ʔu ti sʔuladxʷ. 2. ʔuhədʔiw’d čəd ti sqʷəbayʔ. 3. ʔugʷəč’əd čəɬ
tsi čačas. 4. ʔugʷəč’əb ti čačas. 5. ʔuqʷʷəld ʔu ti sʔuladxʷ. 6. ʔuhədʔiw’b tsi
čačas. 7. ʔuťukʷtxʷ čəɬ ti sqʷəbayʔ. 8. ʔuʔux̌ʷtxʷ. 9. ʔuhədʔiw’d ti sqʷəbayʔ.
10. ʔuqʷʷəld čəɬ ti sʔuladxʷ. 11. ʔugʷəč’əd čəxʷ ʔu ti sqʷəbayʔ. 12. ʔuʔəƛ’txʷ ʔu ti
čačas.

Lesson Four

1. ʔuʔux̌ʷtxʷ tsi luƛ. 2. ʔučubaac čəɬ ti sqigʷac. 3. ʔuʔux̌ʷc ʔu ti sqʷəbayʔ.
4. ʔuʔusil ʔu ti supʼqs. 5. ʔutəlawil ti sqʷəbayʔ. 6. ʔutəlawis čəd ti sqʷəbayʔ.
7. ʔuhədʔiw’txʷ čəxʷ ʔu. 8. ʔuʔəƛ’c čəxʷ ʔu ti luƛ. 9. ʔuɬčis čəɬ.

1. Fish Hawk dove. 2. He dove after a salmon. 3. He took it (up) inland. [Here the most appropriate translation would be, "He carried it up the bank".] 4. He took it home.

Lesson Five

1. ʔucʼəldxʷ čəxʷ ʔu ti ʔaciɬtalbixʷ. 2. ʔubəčad tsi čačas. 3. ʔukʷʷəɬdxʷ čəxʷ ʔu
ti qʷuʔ. 4. ʔuɬčis čəɬ tsi luƛ. 5. ʔuɬalis čələp ʔu ti čačas. 6. ʔutəlawis čəɬ ti
sqʷəbayʔ. 7. ʔuqʷʷəld čələp ʔu ti sʔuladxʷ. 8. ʔuʔəy’dxʷ čəxʷ ʔu ti sqʷəbayʔ.

1. Did you find the dog? 2. I went after the deer. 3. Did someone go [up] away from the water after the child? 4. Did you inadvertently knock the old man over/down? 5. I poured the water. 6. Did you win? 7. Someone took the boy. 8. Did you manage to get a salmon? 9. We put the old woman down. 10. Someone found the old woman.

ʔuɬalis	went ashore after something
ʔuɬalildxʷ	managed to reach shore
ʔuɬaliltxʷ	took someone to shore
ʔuqəɬəd	woke someone up
ʔuqəɬdxʷ	inadvertently woke someone up
ʔukʷəd(d)xʷ	managed to get something
ʔučaldxʷ	caught up with someone
ʔubəčad	set something down
ʔubəčdxʷ	inadvertently knock someone/something over
ʔusaqʷtxʷ	cause something to fly, pilot an airplane
ʔuɬčis	arrived for a particular purpose
ʔuɬčildxʷ	managed to arrive with someone/something
ʔuɬčiltxʷ	arrived with someone/something
ʔutədʸis	went to bed with someone
ʔutədʸiltxʷ	put someone to bed
ʔux̌ʷsild	fattened someone up

Lesson Six

1. ʔuʔəy'dub ʔə ti sqʷəbayʔ ti čačas.	The dog found the boy.
2. ʔutəlawisəb ʔə ti luǰ ti sqʷəbayʔ.	The old man ran after the dog.
3. ʔuhədʔiw'cəb ʔə tsi čačas ti čačas.	The girl went in the house after the boy.
4. ʔugʷəč'təb ʔə tsi čačas tsi luǰ.	The girl looked for the old woman.
5. ʔuʔəǰ'tub ʔə ti luǰ ti ʔaciɬtalbixʷ.	The old man brought the people.

1. ʔuƛ'ukʷtxʷ čəxʷ ʔu tsi luǰ.	Did you take the old woman home?
2. ʔuʔəy'dxʷ čəd ti čačas.	I found the boy.
3. ʔuɬčis čəɬ ti ʔaciɬtalbixʷ.	We arrived to [visit] the people.
4. ʔučubaac čələp ʔu ti luǰ.	Did you folks go inland after the old man?
5. ʔubəčad čəxʷ ʔu tsi luǰ.	Did you put the old woman down?

Lesson Seven

1. (a) The old woman dried the salmon.

   (b) ʔušabalikʷ tsi luǰ ʔə ti sʔuladxʷ. (c) The old woman dried (the) salmon.

2. (a) The people sought spirit power.

(b) ʔugʷəč'əb ti ʔaciɫtalbixʷ ʔə ti sqəlalitut. (c) The people sought spirit power.

3. (a) The boy threw [something] at the dog.

(b) ʔupusil ti č'ač'as ʔə ti č'ƛ̓aʔ. (c) The boy threw a stone/rock.

4. (a) The dog ate the crab.

(b) ʔuʔəɫəd ti sqʷəbayʔ ʔə ti bəsqʷ. (c) The dog ate (the) crab.

5. (a) The old man foraged for (fire)wood.

(b) ʔuʔuləx̌təb ʔə ti luƛ̓ ti hud. (c) The old man came upon and kept the (fire)wood.

6. (a) The girl dug braken fern rhizomes.

(b) ʔuc'aʔtəb ʔə tsi č'ač'as ti sk'ʷiʔxʷ. (c) The girl dug (up) braken fern rhizomes.

7. (a) The boy ate crab.

(b) ʔulək'ʷʷtəb ʔə ti č'ač'as ti bəsqʷ. (c) The boy ate the crab.

8. (a) The old woman cooked/roasted salmon.

(b) ʔuqʷʷəltəb ʔə tsi luƛ̓ ti sʔuladxʷ. (c) The old woman cooked/roasted the salmon.

1. <u>ti sčətxʷəd</u> 2. <u>ʔə ti spčuʔ</u> 3. <u>ti spčuʔ</u> 4. 0 5. <u>ti spčuʔ</u> 6. 0 7. <u>ʔə ti syəcəb</u> 8. <u>ʔə ti ʔulal</u> 9. <u>ti sbiaw</u> 10. <u>ʔə ti č'ƛ̓aʔ</u> 11. <u>ʔə ti sqʷiʔqʷaliʔ</u> 12. <u>ʔə ti č'ƛ̓aʔ</u>.

Lesson Eight

1. ʔukʷədyid čəd ti sqʷəbayʔ ʔə ti šaw. 2. ʔulək'ʷʷyitəb ʔə ti luƛ̓ ʔə ti sʔuladxʷ. 3. ʔuʔəƛ̓'yid ti č'ač'as. 4. ʔuʔəƛ̓'txʷyitəb ʔə tsi č'ač'as tsi luƛ̓. 5. ʔuʔəy'dxʷyid čələp ʔu ti stubš ʔə ti sqʷəbayʔ.

Lesson Nine

1. fed you 2. told me a traditional story 3. got one's self indoors 4. visited me 5. told you about something 6. got one's self into a small and confining place (These answers could as well be in the English present or future tense.)

Lesson Ten

1. ʔəstaqʷuʔ ti sqʷəbayʔ.   2. ʔəstagʷəxʷ čəxʷ ʔu.   3. ʔəsx̌ikʷʷəb ʔu ti lux̌.
4. ʔuɫač'atəb ʔə tsi lux̌ ti hud.   5. ʔuɫiditəb ʔu ʔə ti č'ač'as ti sqʷəbayʔ.   6. ʔəsq'axʷ
ʔu ti stuləkʷ.   7. ʔəslax̌dxʷ čəd.   8. ʔəshiiɫ čəɫ ʔu.   9. ʔəs(h)aydxʷ čəxʷ ʔu tsi č'ač'as.
10. ʔut'ukʷʷtxʷ ti sqʷəbayʔ.   11. ʔukʷʷədatəb ʔu ʔə tsi č'ač'as ti kʷat'aq.   12. ʔəsqʷʷic'
čəd.

Lesson Eleven

II. (1) Typically ləcu- occurs with verbs expressing an activity being done at one place.
(2) ʔəs- expresses a state or condition while ləs- designates a state or condition seen as
contingent upon or intimately involved with a dynamic event.   Most often ləs- refers to
states maintained while moving through space.   (3) An event with the prefix ʔu- is viewed
in its entirety, both its beginning and end.   With ʔu- the event is bounded, while acts with
ləcu- are open ended; the activity is ongoing.   (There is nothing in English quite like ʔu-.)
(4) Patient oriented verbs ending in -d, -t- do not take the prefix lə- (except in its serial
sense).

III.

ʔukʷʷədad	take	ʔut'ilib	sing	ʔutələwil	run
ʔəskʷʷədad	hold	lət'ilib	singing while going along	lətələwil	running
ləcukʷʷədad	carrying in the hand	ləcut'ilib	singing	ləcutələwil	running on a regular basis

Lesson Twelve

1. ʔah ʔu kʷʸi gʷʷəsdəxʷʷiɫs əlgʷʷəʔ.   2. ʔah ʔu kʷʷ(i) gʷʷadbəsqʷ.   3. ʔah ti sčəbid čəɫ.
4. ʔah ʔu kʷʸi gʷʷəqʷʷuʔləp.   5. ʔah ʔu kʷʸi gʷʷadkʷʷat'aq.   6. ʔah ti dhud.   7. ʔah ti
sʔuladxʷ čəɫ.   8. ʔah ti t'isəds əlgʷʷəʔ.

Lesson Thirteen

One: 1. tu-, -ed 2. tu-, -ed 3. tu-, vowel change in English verb 4. x̌u-, would
5. x̌u-, bə-, would, again 6. tu-, -t (and stem changes) 7. tu-, -ed 8. tu-, -ed 9. tu-,
-ed.

Two: 10. ɫu-, will 11. ɫu-, will 12. ɫu-, will 13. tu-, vowel change in English word
14. tu-, vowel change in English verb 15. 0 16. 0.

Three: 17. bə-, again 18. bə-, again 19. bə-, again 20. bə-, more.

Four: 21. ƛ̓u-, would   22. ƛ̓u-, would / ƛ̓u-, habitual   23. gʷə-, no English equivalent (See 12.3b.) / ƛ̓u-, could   24. ƛ̓u-, would   25. ƛ̓u-, 0 / ƛ̓u-, would / bə-, more 26. ɫu-, will / bə-, another   27. ɫu-, will / bə-, back.

Lesson Fourteen

1. ɫu-____ čad ƛ̓uɫ(u)as-_____-əd.   2. ƛ̓uləcu-____ čəxʷ ʔu ɫu-____-əxʷ.   3. ʔu-. čad ɫu-_____-əs.   4. ƛ̓u-____ čəɫ ɫu-____-əɫi.   5. ɫu-____ ____ ɫu- ____ - ə s .
6. _____ ɫu-____-əs.   7. ʔəs-____ čad gʷə-____-əd gʷə-____-əd.
8. _____ ti _____ ʔə ti ___ gʷəs-____-əs.

1. ɫuxʷakʷʷil ƛ̓uɫ(u)astagʷəxʷəs.   2. ƛ̓uləcuƛ̓ilib čəɫ ɫuyayusəɫi.   3. ɫuhikʷ čəxʷ ʔu ɫuluX̣iləxʷ.   4. ʔəsX̣əc čad gʷətəlawiləd.   5. ʔuƛ̓iwiltxʷ ʔu ɫukʷaxʷadəs.   6. p̓aX̣aƛ̓ dxʷʔal dəgʷi gʷəxʷiƛ̓iləɫi.

č̓əlps̲a̲d̲ and xʷəƛ̓’s̲a̲d̲; *ankle, leg.*

Lesson Fifteen

1. ʔuč̓aʔtəb ʔə ti dsqʷəbayʔ tiʔəʔ šaw. [or] ʔuč̓aʔəb ti dsqʷəbayʔ ʔə tiʔəʔ šaw. 2. ʔugʷəč̓əb tsiʔəʔ č̓ač̓as ʔə tiʔiɫ. [or] ʔugʷəč̓’təb ʔə tsiʔəʔ č̓ač̓as tiʔiɫ.   3. ʔuʔəƛ̓’txʷ čəɫ tiʔəʔ sqʷəbayʔ.   4. ʔuʔəƛ̓’tubuɫ tsiʔiɫ sɫadəyʔ. [or] ʔuʔəƛ̓’tub čəɫ ʔə tiʔiɫ sɫadəyʔ. 5. ʔukʷʷəɫdxʷ tiʔəʔ q̓uʔ.   6. ʔukʷʷədatəb ʔə tiʔiɫ stubš ti dsqʷəbayʔ.   7. ʔuɫač̓dxʷ čələp ʔu (ti hud).   8. ʔuʔabyid ti sqʷəbayʔs ʔə tə šaw. (All of these sentences could have begun with tu- instead of ʔu-. From the Lushootseed perspective all of the English sentences from which these are translated are ambiguous in this matter.)

Lesson Sixteen

1. predicate - augment - adjunct: It was spread up toward yonder house.

2. predicate - oblique complement - direct complement - adjunct: The boy threw a rock at this dog.

3. predicate - adjunct: [Someone] is walking by the (lit., this) shore of the sea/sound.

4. predicate - augment: [Someone] is walking by the shore.

5. predicate - direct complement: This is a rock.

6. predicate - oblique complement: This cat took [something].

7. predicate - adjunct: [Someone] threw the rock.

8. predicate - direct complement: [Someone] took a hold of this cat.

9. predicate - oblique complement - adjunct: The old man gave [someone] the dog.

10. predicate - adjunct: [Someone] ate crab.

11. predicate - direct complement: [Someone] cooked the salmon.

12. predicate - direct complement - adjunct: [Someone] gave the dog to the boy.

13. predicate - adjunct: [Someone] cooked the salmon.

14. predicate - direct complement - adjunct - adjunct: The woman dug braken fern rhizomes over there.

Lesson Seventeen

1. ʔəsx̌əɬ čəxʷ ʔu. Are you sick? 2. həlaʔb čəxʷ ʔu ʔəsx̌əɬ. Are you really sick? 3. ckʷʷaqid sixʷ x̌ʷulʼ ʔuʔəɬəd. [He/she] is always simply eating. 4. ʔəsx̌əɬ uʔxʷ čəxʷ ʔu. Are you still sick? 5. x̌ub čəɬ ʔu x̌ʷulʼ ɬutʼukʷ. Should we just go home?

Lesson Eighteen

1. You didn't go. 2. That's not the one. / He, she is not it. 3. It is not really food. 4. Maybe it won't rain. 5. Don't you let me fall off. 6. I don't have [any] money. 7. I don't really eat a lot. (More literally: It is not really a lot that I eat.) 8. It isn't mine.

Lesson Nineteen

1a. This cat ate the salmon. b. sʔuladxʷ ti ʔulək̓ʷtəb ʔə tiʔəʔ pišpiš. c. pišpiš ti ʔulək̓ʷəd ti sʔuladxʷ. 2a. This man tied this shovel-nose canoe. b. x̌əlayʔ tiʔəʔ ʔuɬiditəb ʔə tiʔəʔ stubš. c. stubš tiʔəʔ ʔuɬidid tiʔəʔ x̌əlayʔ. 3a. Those children threw [something] at this dog. b. sqʷəbayʔ tiʔiɬ ʔupusutəb ʔə tiʔiɬ wiwʼsu. c. wiwʼsu tiʔiɬ ʔupusud tiʔəʔ sqʷəbayʔ. 4a. This dog chased those children. b. wiwʼsu ti ʔučalatəb ʔə tiʔəʔ sqʷəbayʔ. c. sqʷəbayʔ ti ʔučalad tiʔiɬ wiwʼsu.

Part III.

1. stab k̓ʷi ʔuʔəx̌ʼtub ʔə ts(i) adskʷuy. 2. gʷat k̓ʷi ʔudᶻubud t(i) adsqʷəbayʔ. 3. gʷat k̓ʷi ʔux̌əx̌təb ʔə ti sqʷəbayʔ čəɬ. 4. gʷat k̓ʷi ʔudᶻubucid. 5. stab k̓ʷi ʔuʔəyʼdxʷ čəxʷ. 6. gʷat k̓ʷi ʔukʷaxʷad čəxʷ. 7. stab k̓ʷi ʔux̌əcdxʷ ti sqʷəbayʔs. 8. gʷat k̓ʷi ʔudᶻubutəb ʔə ti stiqiw.

Lesson Twenty

1. Where did you put (lit. set down) the ladle? 2. It was a salmon that the cat ate. 3. It was the cat that ate the salmon. 4. Where did he put the paddle? 5. Stones were what the children were tossing. 6. That is (the place) where I got my food.

1. Patient suffix forming a goal oriented stem. 2. Third person suffix marking an agent oriented verb when preceded by an adjunct. 3. Third person suffix marking the patient of a -t-əb verb when preceded by an adjunct. 4. Patient suffix forming a goal oriented stem. 5. Third person suffix marking an agent of a patient oriented (but not -t-əb) when preceded by an adjunct. 6. Third person suffix marking an agent of a patient (but not -t-əb) verb when preceded by an interrogative adjunct.

Lesson Twenty-One

I. 1. habitual 2. habitual 3. jussive 4. habitual 5. conditional 6. habitual 7. fear; habitual 8. conditional 9. conditional 10. conditional

II. 1. 21.5a: ʔukʷəd(d)xʷ <u>tiʔił spusutəbs tiʔəʔ wiw̓su</u>.

2. 21.5c: dił <u>tiʔəʔ cəxʷkʷəd(d)xʷ tiʔəʔ dsʔəłəd</u>.

3. 21.5b: dᶻux̌ʷatəxʷ <u>ʔə tiʔəʔ p̓q̓ac tusuʔəłəds</u>.

4. 21.5b: x̌ʷul' čəxʷ ləʔux̌ʷ <u>dxʷʔal kʷ(i) adsłčil</u>.

5. 21.6a: ʔukʷədad tiʔəʔ qʷuʔ <u>dəxʷuc̓agʷači(ʔ)b</u> ʔal tiʔəʔ sbałs.

5. 21.5b: ʔukʷədad tiʔəʔ qʷuʔ dəxʷuc̓agʷačiʔb <u>ʔal tiʔəʔ sbałs</u>.

6. 21.5a: x̌ʷul' čəd łuləʔux̌ʷtxʷ <u>tiʔəʔ ł(u)adsʔəłtxʷ əlgʷəʔ</u>.

III. There are **six** clauses. x̌ʷiʔəxʷ. **One** has the clitic pattern. (kʷi) łudəxʷhuydxʷs.

łuhuydxʷ čəxʷ kʷ(i) adsləkʷʷdxʷ / a(d)dəxʷləkʷʷdxʷ tiʔəʔ dsʔuladxʷ.

(Or simply, łuləkʷʷdxʷ čəxʷ tiʔəʔ dsʔuladxʷ.)

(Or, łuləkʷʷdxʷyic čəd tiʔəʔ (d)sʔuladxʷ.)

TEXTS

TEXTS

The following graphic devices used in representing these texts need explanation:

1. Brackets, [ ], enclose editorial additions. This material is not on the tape recording on which the transcription is based.

2. As mentioned in the grammar, parentheses, ( ), surround a letter that stands for a part of a word which is not pronounced in certain situations. See, for example, 13.7b in the grammar section.

3. Words or parts of words written between angles, < >, represent false starts, slips of the tongue, etc., and are to be ignored. (Some people might wonder why some words or parts of words heard on the tape do not appear in the written version, so such slips of the tongue are marked in these texts in this manner.)

4. The period, . , marks the conclusion of a main clause and whatever subordinate clauses or other modifying elements go with it. All such units can be and often are complete sentences. However, many times speakers string together in a single breath group two or more such clauses without letting the voice pitch fall between them. These breath groups (i.e., intonational contours or 'phonological sentences' as opposed to 'grammatical sentences') are not indicated in the first four texts, however, because in these stories the end of the clause and breath group are essentially congruent.

5. An attempt has been made to draw the readers' attention to a part of the structure inherent in good Lushootseed storytelling by grouping the lines into units. However, it should be pointed out that this structure is more artfully developed in some stories than others. Furthermore, for the texts included here, analysis of style has thus far been neglected in favor of close attention to accuracy in transcription and gloss. Therefore, readers should not doubt their own ideas about appropriate divisions simply because these might differ from those presented here.

bibščəb ʔi tiʔił suʔsuqʷaʔs, tətyika
Young Mink and Tutyeeka

Narrator's introductory remarks:

1. ʔah dəgʷi, siʔab dsyaʔyaʔ.

2. tux̌ʷəxʷ čəd łuyəhubtubicid, ti tusyəhub ʔə tu·diʔ tusluX̌luX̌ čəł.

3. tuyəcəbtub čəd ʔə tiʔił tudyəl'yəlab.

4. hay čəd łuyəcəbtubicidəxʷ, dəgʷi siʔab dsyaʔyaʔ.

5. tiʔił bibščəb ʔi tiʔił suʔsuqʷaʔs, tətyika, tiʔił łudsyəhubtubicid.

Story begins here:

6. hay, ʔułiʔłda(hə)b tiʔił bibščəb ʔi tiʔił suʔsuqʷaʔs, tətyika.

7. ʔułiʔłda(hə)b əlgʷəʔ.

8. huy, šudx̌ʷəxʷ tiʔił čx̌ʷəluʔ.

9. huy, bapadəxʷ əlgʷəʔ.

10. bapadəxʷ əlgʷəʔ tiʔił čx̌ʷəluʔ.

11. huy, x̌ʷak̓ʷisəbəxʷ ʔə tiʔił čx̌ʷəluʔ.

12. huy, bəq̓təbaxʷ ʔə tiʔił čx̌ʷəluʔ.

13. łixʷ[əł]dat[43] tiʔił [s]dəgʷabacil[s]əxʷ əlgʷəʔ ʔə tiʔił čx̌ʷəluʔ.

14. huy, ʔibibəšəxʷ tiʔił bibščəb.

15. ʔibibəšəxʷ.

16. huy, k̓awdx̌ʷəxʷ tiʔił sc̓aliʔ ʔə tiʔił čx̌ʷəluʔ.

17. 'ʔuʔəx̌ix̌ədəxʷ čəxʷ, bibščəb.'

---

[43]In a traditional story from Northern Lushootseed one would expect buusəłdat *four days* because four -- not three -- is the traditional number. Events usually happen four times, often there are four brothers in a story, etc. By speaking of three rather than four days, Mr. Sam has made a small adaptation to Western Culture. (In Southern Lushootseed the traditional number is five rather than four.)

18. '?u·, tux̌ʷ čəd ?u?ibibəš.'

19. 'bibščəb. x̌ʷi? k̓ʷi [gʷ]adsuk̓awdx̌ʷ ti?ił [ds]c̓ali?.'

20. huy, cutəx̌ʷ ti?ił bibščəb,

21. '?u·.'

22. hay, gʷadadgʷadəx̌ʷ ti?ił bibščəb ?i ti?ił su?suqʷa?s, tətyika.

23. 'ƛ̓ub čəł ?uhudčup čła k̓ʷuk̓ʷcut.'

24. huy, hudčupəx̌ʷ əlgʷə?.

25. '?u?əx̌ix̌ədəx̌ʷ čəx̌ʷ, bibščəb.'

26. '?u·, tux̌ʷ čəd ?uhudčup.'

27. huy, łič̓itəbəx̌ʷ ti?ił s.c̓ali? ?ə ti?ił čx̌ʷəlu?.

28. '?u?əx̌ix̌ədəx̌ʷ čəx̌ʷ, bibščəb.'

29. day̓ ?uhaydub ?ə ti?ił čx̌ʷəlu?.

30. huy, tu?ux̌ʷəx̌ʷ ti?ił čx̌ʷəlu?.

31. ti·ləb dx̌ʷt̓aq̓t ti?ił słalil ?ə ti?ił čx̌ʷəlu?.

32. dadatu[t] ti?ił sk̓ʷilil ?ə ti?ił bibščəb.

33. ?uluud ti?ił luƛ̓ tudi? t̓aq̓t.

34. ləcup̓ayəq ?ə ti?ił sdi?dəxʷił.

35. huy, t̓ilibəx̌ʷ ti?ił bibščəb.

36. t̓ilibəx̌ʷ,

37.   'stab čəx̌ʷ stab ?uk̓ʷixʷid. stab čəx̌ʷ stab ?uk̓ʷixʷid.

38.   hagʷəx̌ʷ čəd tu?acigʷədil ?ə tə luƛ̓ čx̌ʷəlu?, čx̌ʷəlu?.

39.   stab čəx̌ʷ stab ?uk̓ʷixʷid. stab čəx̌ʷ stab ?uk̓ʷixʷid.

40.   hagʷəx̌ʷ čəd tu?acigʷədil ?ə tə luƛ̓ čx̌ʷəlu?, čx̌ʷəlu?.'

41. huy, təlawiləx̌ʷ ti?ił luƛ̓.

42. huy, yəcəbax̌ʷ ?ə ti?ił bibščəb ?i ti?ił su?suqʷa?s, tətyika, ?ə ti?ił słaliltubsəx̌ʷ.

43. huy, ?ux̌ʷəx̌ʷ tə ?aciłtalbixʷ.

44. bəčatəbəxʷ tiʔił kʷatʼaq dəxʷʔibəš ʔə tiʔił bibščəb ʔi tiʔił suʔsuqʷaʔs.

45. puˑtəxʷ ʔəsłuqʷač tiʔił bibščəb ʔi tiʔił suʔsuqʷaʔs, tətyika.[44]

46. huy, tʼukʷtubəxʷ tiʔił bibščəb ʔi tiʔił suʔsuqʷaʔs.

47. huy, qʷuʔtəbəxʷ tiʔił ʔaciłtalbixʷ tuˑlʔal bəkʷ čad.

48. huy, ʔəłtub tə ʔaciłtalbixʷ.

49. huy gʷəl, ĵuʔiləxʷ tə ʔaciłtalbixʷ.

50. huy, higʷiləxʷ siʔab tiʔił bibščəb ʔi tiʔił suʔsuqʷaʔs, tətyika.

51. huyəxʷ tiʔił dsyəhub[tubi]cid, siʔab dsyaʔyaʔ.

52. huyəxʷ čəd.

---

[44]In the old days raconteurs seldom told a story the same way every time. They altered the emphasis according to the occasion and audience. Episodes were expanded or reduced, often omitted as suited the purpose of a particular story session. Sometimes as here an episode is reduced to a single line. Because the audience had heard these stories all their lives, they did not need to know what had happened to Mink's and Tutyeeka's hair for they already knew. In some other telling that incident is developed when judged important to the occasion. (In Southern Lushootseed, by the way, Mink is named for his bald head, cʼəbalqid.)

sčətxʷəd ʔi tsiʔiɬ X̌aX̌acʼapəd

Bear and Ant

1. hay, ʔah tiʔəʔ syəyəhub ʔə tiʔiɬ sčətxʷəd ʔi tsiʔiɬ X̌aX̌acʼapəd.

2. tiʔəʔ sčətxʷəd gʷəl x̌ʷu·lʼ X̌uʔibibəš.

3. x̌ʷu·lʼ X̌uʔibibəš.

4. gʷəl tsiʔiɬ X̌aX̌acʼapəd gʷəl dˑəgʷaʔ dxʷʔulus.

5. hay, ʔaliləxʷ čəd tiʔəʔ sčətxʷəd.

6. X̌iqagʷiləxʷ tiʔiɬ sčətxʷəd tulʼʔal tiʔiɬ ʔalʔals.

7. tiʔiɬ ʔalʔals X̌udəxʷʔux̌ʷs ʔal tiʔiɬ pə(d)tʼəs.

8. X̌iqagʷil tiʔiɬ sčətxʷəd.

9. huy, ʔibibəšəxʷ.

10. ʔibibəšəxʷ.

11. gʷəčʼəbaxʷ.

12. stab kʷi gʷəsuʔəɬəds.

13. gʷəl ʔah kʷaʔ tsi[ʔiɬ] X̌aX̌acʼapəd.

14. ləcuyayus, ləcuyayus, ləcuyayus, ckʷaqid ləcuyayus.

15. ʔuqʷuʔəd tiʔiɬ stab gʷədəxʷ(h)əliʔis(s) əlgʷəʔ,
    <ɬdəxʷuʔəɬəds>
    stab gʷədəxʷuʔəɬəds əlgʷəʔ,
    stab gʷ[s]uʔəyʼdxʷ[s].

16. ləcuqʷuʔəd tiʔiɬ sʔəɬəds əlgʷəʔ.

17. gʷəl X̌uʔaʔild əlgʷəʔ [tiʔiɬ] ɬudəxʷʔa(h)s kʷi stab ɬus[u]ʔəɬəds əlgʷəʔ.

18. ʔah kʷaʔ tiʔəʔ sčətxʷəd.

19. x̌ʷulʼ ləcuʔibibəš.

20. x̌ʷulʼ ləcuʔiʔɬadəb ʔə tiʔəʔ sqʷəlaɬəd ʔə tiʔiɬ X̌usqʷəls.

21. ʔa·h gʷəl X̌ubəɬaxʷ tiʔiɬ sčətxʷəd.

22. pu·təxʷ x̌(u)asbəɫ!

23. hay gʷəl x̌uʔux̌ʷəxʷ.

24. gʷəl x̌[u]dxʷpakʷahəbəxʷ.

25. hay gʷəl x̌uʔitutəxʷ.

26. huy, x̌ax̌iləxʷ t[s]iʔəʔ x̌ax̌acʼapəd ʔi tiʔiɫ sčətxʷəd.

27. x̌ax̌iləxʷ əlgʷəʔ.

28. huy, qʷʼuʔtəbəxʷ tiʔiɫ bəkʷʼaʔkʷbixʷ.

29. [s]əsqʷʼuʔs əlgʷəʔ.

30. qʷʼuʔtəbəxʷ tiʔiʔiɫ siʔiʔab.

31. <gʷəl> huy, gʷadadgʷadəxʷ əlgʷəʔ gʷəgʷatəs kʷi ɫucʼəlalikʷ.

32. wiliqʷʼitəbəxʷ tsiʔəʔ x̌ax̌acʼapəd gʷəsčaləs kʷi x̌əčs.

33. huy cutəxʷ:

34.   ɫax̌il gʷəl bələx̌il. ɫax̌il gʷəl bələx̌il. ɫax̌il gʷəl bələx̌i·l.
        ɫax̌il gʷəl bələx̌il. ɫax̌il gʷəl bələx̌il. ɫax̌il gʷəl bələx̌i·l.
        we· xʷeʔe·ʔ. ...e·.

        ɫax̌il gʷəl bələx̌il. ɫax̌il gʷəl bələx̌il. ɫax̌il gʷəl bələx̌il.
        we· xʷeʔe·ʔ. ... e·.

35. gʷəl ʔəsčal tiʔəʔ sčətxʷəd.

36. x̌ʷulʼ ʔəxʷpakʷ[ah]əb tiʔiɫ sčətxʷəd.

37. x̌ʷulʼ x̌[u]bəxʷpusəb.

38. gʷəl x̌[u]bəcut:

39. dukʷəla·dxʷ gʷəl ɫubələx̌i·l.

40. diɫ dayʼ x̌uscut ʔə tiʔiɫ sčətxʷəd.

41. huy ʔəsqʷicʼ.

42. hay gʷəl <tac> x̌ʷulʼəxʷ x̌ubədᶻubalikʷ[45] tsiʔiɫ x̌ax̌acʼapəd.

---

[45]The word actually used by Mr. Sam was tac a word borrowed from English *dance*.
In this text a native Lushootseed word has been substituted, namely, dᶻubalik. (This latter

43. putəxʷ x̌[u]bəx̌acʼahəb tsiʔił x̌ax̌acʼapəd.

44. x̌ʷul' x̌[u]bəxʷpusəb tiʔəʔ sčətxʷəd.

45. gʷəl x̌[u]bəcut:

46. dukʷəla·dxʷ gʷəl ł[u]bələx̌i·l.

47. dił day̓ x̌uscut ʔə tiʔił sčətxʷəd.

48. hay, putəxʷ x̌[u]bətʼilib <tiʔəʔ sčətxʷəd> tsiʔəʔ x̌ax̌acʼapəd.

49. x̌ʷu·l'əxʷ x̌[u]bətʼilib.

50. pu·təxʷ x̌[u]bəx̌acʼahəb.

51. hay, gʷəl x̌[u]bətʼilibəxʷ:

52.
    łax̌il gʷəl bələx̌il.   łax̌il gʷəl bələx̌il.

    łax̌il gʷəl bələx̌il.   łax̌il gʷəl bələx̌il.

    łax̌il gʷəl bələx̌il.   łax̌il gʷəl bələx̌il.

    łax̌il gʷəl bələx̌il.   łax̌il gʷəl bələx̌il. heʔehe··   ʔa· . . .

53. <hay, gʷəl cʼəlalikʷəxʷ tiʔəʔ sčətxʷəd.>

54. hay, tuʔabyitəbəxʷ ʔə tiʔił x̌aʔx̌aʔ <tiʔił> [ʔə kʷi dił] stab[s kʷi] gʷəsx̌ax̌'s.

55. gʷəl ʔah kʷaʔ tiʔəʔ sčətxʷəd.

56. pu·təxʷ ʔəsbəł.

57. put x̌[u]bəʔitut tiʔił ʔəxʷpakʷahəb.

58. cʼəlalikʷ tsiʔił x̌ax̌acʼapəd.

59. pu·təxʷ ʔəxʷx̌əcqgʷas tsiʔəʔ x̌ax̌acʼapəd.

60. gʷəl' cʼəlalikʷ.

61. cʼəlalikʷ huy dxʷʔulus.

62. ckʷaqid x̌uyayus.

---

word is built on the root dᶻub(u) meaning *kick*.)

63. hay, dᶻubalikʷəxʷ[46] tsiʔəʔ x̌ax̌acʼapəd.

64. ʔəshiiɬ.

65.   ɬax̌il gʷəl bələx̌il.   ɬax̌il gʷəl bələx̌il.
      ɬax̌il gʷəl bələx̌il.   ɬax̌il gʷəl bələx̌il.
      ɬax̌il gʷəl bələx̌il.   ɬax̌il gʷəl bələx̌il.
      ɬax̌il gʷəl bələx̌il.   ɬax̌il gʷəl bələx̌il.
      we· xʷeʔe·ʔ.   we· xʷeʔe·ʔ.

[66. diɬ shuys.]

---

[46]The information in footnote 45 applies here also.

sbiaw ʔi tiʔił hikʷ čፘaʔ

Coyote and the Big Rock

1. ʔuʔux̌ʷ tiʔəʔ sbiaw.

2. gʷəl ʔuʔəy'dxʷ tiʔił ʔiišəds.

3. ʔušudxʷ tiʔił səsqʷuʔ ʔə tiʔił ʔiišəds ʔal tiʔəʔ hikʷ čፘaʔ.

4. put ʔəsp'il šqabac tiʔəʔ hikʷ čፘaʔ.

5. hay gʷəl [ʔu]wiliqʷidəxʷ tiʔił ʔiišəds,

6. 'stab tiʔił suhuyləp.'

7. 'ʔu·, tux̌ʷ čəł ʔəsqʷuʔ.

8. ləcuʔabyid čəł tiʔəʔ čፘaʔ ʔə tiʔəʔ stabigʷs čəł,

9. tiʔəʔ łusʔibəš čəł.

10. hay gʷəl łuhuyutəbəxʷ čit tiʔił dəxʷʔibəš čəł.

11. dił dəxʷut'asad čəł tiʔəʔ čፘaʔ.'

12. hay gʷəl cutəxʷ tiʔəʔ sbiaw,

13. 'hay čəda łuqʷibid.

14. x̌ʷul' p'aፘaፘ tiʔəʔ dsʔabyid.'

15. huy,[ʔu]pačad tiʔił stabigʷs sʔabyid[s].

16. huy, kʷatajəxʷ tiʔił sbiaw ʔə tiʔił čፘaʔ.

17. huy ʔabyidəxʷ ʔə tiʔił x̌ʷu·l' p'aፘaፘ stab.

18. gʷəl xʷiʔ [kʷi] gʷədəxʷ(h)aʔłs.

19. hay gʷəl xʷt'agʷiləxʷ tiʔił sbiaw.

20. x̌ayəb tiʔił sbiaw,

21. 'stab əw'ə tiʔəʔ čፘaʔ cəxʷyaw' ʔut'asbil.'

22. hay gʷəl [ʔu]ʔibəšəxʷ tiʔił sbiaw.

23. gʷəl tiʔił sʔuxʷ ʔə tiʔił sʔibəšs.⁴⁷

24. gʷəl [ʔu]luudəxʷ tiʔił stab.

25. ləcutukʷucut.

26. [ʔu]dᶻalqʷusəxʷ tiʔił sbiaw.

27. gʷəl [ʔu]šudxʷəxʷ tiʔił hikʷ čƛ̕aʔ.

28. ləcučalad tiʔił sbiaw.

29. hi·kʷ ləcutukʷucut ʔə tiʔił sətəčs ʔə tiʔił sčalads tiʔił sbiaw.

30. ʔəsx̌icil tiʔił čƛ̕aʔ ʔə tiʔił sučalads tiʔił sbiaw.

31. yəx̌i huy x̌ʷiʔ [kʷi] gʷəstab [gʷə]dəxʷ(h)aʔł[s].

32. x̌ʷul' p̓aƛ̕aƛ̕ tiʔił sʔabyids tiʔił čƛ̕aʔ.

33. huy, [lə]təlawiləxʷ tiʔəʔ sbiaw.

34. təla·wiləxʷ.

35. huy, [lə]čalatəb ʔə tiʔił čƛ̕aʔ.

36. hay, [ʔu]wiliqʷidəxʷ tiʔił suqʷsuqʷaʔs,

37. 'stabəxʷ [kʷi] łudshuy [tiʔiʔəʔ] dsuqʷsuqʷaʔ.

38. [ʔəs]c'udəxʷ čəd.

39. x̌ʷakʷiləxʷ čəd.'

40. hay gʷəl cutəxʷ tiʔił suqʷsuqʷaʔs,

41. gʷəl 'cutəxʷ čəx ̌ sixʷ, 'haʔkʷ čəd ʔəxʷcutəb'.'

42. x̌ʷul' čəxʷ ʔugʷəč'əb ʔə kʷi stab, [s]əsliʔluʔ ʔə tiʔił sbadil čxʷa šulagʷil.

43. ʔəsmiʔman'.

44. x̌ʷiʔ [kʷi] gʷədəxʷšulagʷildubut ʔə tiʔił čƛ̕aʔ.'

45. tiʔił sbiaw gʷəl [ʔu]ʔuxʷəxʷ.

46. [ʔu]dəgʷagʷiləxʷ ʔə tiʔił [s]əsliʔluʔ.

---

⁴⁷Line 23 is actually a nominalized subordinate clause that goes with line 24. It is unusual in that it precedes rather than follows its main clause. The double use of gʷəl is reminiscent of topicalization (22.8b). A suggested rendering in English of lines 23 and 24 is the following: *And while his journey went [along], he heard something.*

47. hay gʷəl [ʔu]čalatəb ʔə tiʔił čX̌aʔ.

48. x̌ʷiʔ [kʷi] gʷəshədʔiw'dubuts.⁴⁸

49. huy, [ʔu]dᶻəlqcutəxʷ tiʔił čX̌aʔ dxʷʔal tiʔił [s]əsluʔ.

50. gʷəl cuucəxʷ tiʔił sbiaw,

51. 'łuʔa·(h) čəxʷ [tiʔił] x̌ʷul' ł(u)adsyubil.'

52. gʷəl ha·gʷəxʷ tiʔił sʔa··(h) ʔə tiʔił sbiaw.

53. pu·təxʷ t(u)asX̌uX̌uil tiʔił sbiaw.

54. putəxʷ t(u)asX̌uil.

55. gʷəl [ʔu]lax̌dxʷ tiʔił suqʷsuqʷaʔs.

56. hay, 'X̌iqagʷil ti dsuqʷsuqʷaʔ.

57. ʔəsc'u·dəxʷ čəd.

58. stabəxʷ [kʷi] łudshuy.

59. stabəxʷ [kʷi] łu[d]shuy, ti dsuqʷsuqʷaʔ.'

60. hay gʷəl [ʔu]X̌iqagʷiləxʷ tiʔił suqʷsuqʷaʔs.

61. gʷəl 'cutəxʷ čəxʷ sixʷ, 'haʔkʷ čəd ʔəxʷcutəb'.

62. x̌ʷul' čəxʷ ʔuq'əwab čxʷa [ʔu]xʷəbəbxʷəbaladi(ʔ)b.

63. hay gʷəl gʷə[xʷ]cutəbəxʷ tiʔił čX̌aʔ,

64. 'ʔu·, hikʷ əw'ə qa(h) tiʔił ʔiišəd ʔə tiʔił sbiaw.'

65. 'ʔuʔəx̌ix̌ədəxʷ čəxʷ sbiaw.'

66. 'ʔu·, tux̌ʷ čəd ləcuqʷuʔəd tə dʔiišəd.'

67. huy [ʔu]x̌ədᶻaxʷ⁴⁹ tiʔił čX̌aʔ.

68. huy ʔux̌ʷəxʷ.

69. łəgʷłəxʷ tiʔił sbiaw.

70. [ʔu]cut tiʔił sbiaw.

---

⁴⁸In more precise usage one would expect dəkʷ- or šul- instead of hədʔiw'-.

⁴⁹The stem of this word is actually x̌əc. The final c becomes dᶻ under the influence of the following stressed vowel.

71. [ʔu]x̌ayəb.

72. 'dəgʷagʷil łi dsuqʷsuqʷaʔ.

73. haʔkʷ čəd ʔəxʷcutəb.'

74. huy tuc̓əlalikʷ tiʔił sbiaw.

75. [ʔu]c̓əldəxʷ tiʔił hikʷ č̓x̌aʔ.

76. dił sc̓əldxʷs.

77. 'dəgʷagʷil łi dsuqʷsuqʷaʔ.

78. haʔkʷ čəd ʔəxʷcutəb.'

79. diłəxʷ.

80. huyəxʷ <ʔə> tiʔəʔ dsyəcəb, siʔab dsyaʔyaʔ.

sčətxʷəd ʔi tiʔiɬ c'ix̌c'ix̌
Bear and Fish Hawk

1. ʔa(h) tiʔiɬ sčətxʷəd ʔal kʷədiʔ dəxʷəsɬaɬlils.

2. hay gʷəl tulax̌dxʷəxʷ tiʔiɬ syaʔyaʔs.

3. gʷəl tuʔux̌ʷcəxʷ.

4. gʷəl tudᶻəlax̌adbidəxʷ tiʔiɬ x̌ibx̌ib, c'ix̌c'ix̌ tiʔiɬ həlaʔb sdaʔs, c'ix̌c'ix̌.

5. gʷəl tudᶻəlax̌adbid ʔal tiʔiɬ pə(d)t'əs.

6. huy gʷəl tuʔux̌ʷc⁵⁰ tiʔiɬ syaʔyaʔs.

7. lax̌dxʷ<bid>əxʷ.

8. hay gʷəl cut(t)əbəxʷ tiʔəʔ c'ix̌c'ix̌,

9. ʔəstagʷəxʷəxʷ tiʔiɬ syaʔyaʔs, sčətxʷəd.

10. hay, tukʷit'əxʷ ʔal tiʔiɬ stuləkʷ.

11. [ʔu]saqʷ dxʷšəq tiʔiɬ c'ix̌c'ix̌.

12. gʷəl tušudxʷ tiʔiɬ sʔuladxʷ ʔal tiʔiɬ sq'axʷ.

13. gʷəl⁵¹ tuʔusis.

14. gʷəl tukʷəd(d)xʷ tiʔəʔ sʔuladxʷ.

15. tučubətxʷəxʷ.

16. hay, tukʷukʷcutəxʷ⁵² ʔal tiʔiɬ syaʔyaʔs, sčətxʷəd.

17. hay gʷəl tuhədhədači(ʔ)bəxʷ tiʔəʔ c'ix̌c'ix̌,

18. 'c'i·x̌əb, c'ix̌əb, c'ix̌əb, c'ix̌əb.'

---

⁵⁰This is Mr. Sam's amended version. On tape he says, "huy, ʔux̌ʷ dxʷʔal tiʔiɬ syaʔyaʔ."

⁵¹Here this word is pronounced [gʷa··l].

⁵²The root, i.e., core, of this word is one of the rare loan words from English, namely, *cook*. The rest of the sentence also shows 'foreign' language influence. In standard Lushootseed it would be, tuq'ʷəlyid tiʔiɬ syaʔyaʔs, sčətxʷəd.

19. hay gʷəl [ʔu]ʔabyidəxʷ tiʔił sčətxʷəd [ʔə tiʔił bəsx̌ʷəs]

20. gʷəl dəxʷc'ibs ʔə tiʔił sʔuladxʷ ʔə tiʔił bəsx̌ʷəs.⁵³

21. hay gʷəl tusulayitəbəxʷ ʔə tiʔił saliʔ sqʷiqʷəlałəd.

22. hay, ʔəłəd tiʔəʔ sčətxʷəd.

23. ʔal suʔəłəds ʔə tiʔił sʔuladxʷs gʷəl x̌ʷi·ʔ k̓ʷi gʷəsbək̓ʷdxʷs.

24. hay, dxʷx̌ʷal'igʷədəxʷ.

25. ʔušuuc tiʔił sqʷəlałəd.

26. saʔ saliʔ sqʷəlałəd.⁵⁴

27. gʷəl ʔəsqʷu(ʔ)bidəxʷ.

28. huy, tuʔəłədaxʷ.

29. k̓ʷədad tiʔəʔ dəč'uʔ.

30. hi·k̓ʷ tuhaʔł tiʔił sqʷəlałəd.

31. hay gʷəl k̓ʷədadəxʷ.

32. gʷəl ʔəs(h)aydxʷəxʷ x̌ʷiʔəxʷ.

33. huy, saʔsəliʔ.

34. hay gʷəl bəšuł.

35. bəʔa·(h) tiʔił sqʷəlałəd.

36. huy, yəlači(ʔ)bidəxʷ tiʔił sʔəłəd.

37. gʷəl ʔəłəd, ʔəłəd, ʔəłəd, ʔi··· ʔubəł.

38. gʷəl dxʷx̌ʷal'igʷəd.

39. gʷəl huyəxʷ.

40. gʷəl ʔah uʔxʷ tiʔił sʔəłəd.

41. huy, cuucəxʷ tiʔił syaʔyaʔs, c̓ix̌c̓ix̌,

42. 'day̓ čəxʷ łuʔəƛ̓ dxʷʔal tiʔił dʔalʔal čəda łuʔəłtubicid.

---

⁵³Line 20 is a nominalized subordinate clause of line 19. It has been given semi-independent status by being introduced by gʷəl. Compare this line with 23 in the preceding story.

⁵⁴Literally this line says, *"[The] two berries are/were bad."* What it actually means is, *"[Bear thought,] 'There are only two insignificant [or 'measly'] berries.'"*

43. [ɬu]dᶻəlax̌adbic čəxʷ.'

44. huy, cut tiʔiɬ c̓ix̌c̓ix̌,

45. 'x̌ʷub.'

46. hay lax̌d[ubəxʷ ʔə]⁵⁵ tiʔiɬ c̓ix̌c̓ix̌ <ʔə> tiʔiɬ tuscut(t)əbs ʔə tiʔiɬ sčətxʷəd,

47. 'dᶻəlax̌adbic.'

48. hay tuʔux̌ʷəxʷ.

49. gʷəl dxʷtəyiləxʷ ʔə tiʔiɬ stuləkʷ.

50. ʔah tiʔiɬ sčətxʷəd ʔəstədᶻil.

51. gʷəl ɬčisəb ʔə tiʔiɬ ʔay̓əds, c̓ix̌c̓ix̌.

52. gʷa·dadgʷadəxʷ əlgʷəʔ.

53. hay gʷəl ʔəxʷcutəbəxʷ tiʔəʔ sčətxʷəd.

54. 'x̌al̓ čəd gʷəbəʔuləx̌yid tiʔəʔ c̓ix̌c̓ix̌ ʔə kʷi sʔuladxʷ.'

55. kʷit̓əxʷ dxʷča?kʷ ʔal tiʔəʔ stuləkʷ.

56. šuɬəxʷ <tiʔəʔ ča?kʷ> tiʔəʔ sčətxʷəd ʔal tiʔəʔ stuləkʷ.

57. tiʔiɬ ti sʔuladxʷ.

58. saxʷəbid ʔal tiʔəʔ sq̓axʷ.

59. x̌ʷul̓ ʔuq̓cač tiʔiɬ sčətxʷəd.

60. gʷəl ʔugʷət̓q̓ʷad.

61. hay, ʔux̌ʷ.

62. čəba?təbəxʷ ʔə tiʔəʔ sya?ya?s, c̓ix̌c̓ix̌.

63. gʷəl ʔux̌ʷtubəxʷ dxʷʔal tiʔiɬ ʔalʔals.

64. hay gʷəl qəɬ tiʔiɬ sčətxʷəd.

65. ʔahəxʷ tiʔiɬ sʔuladxʷ.

66. tuʔux̌ʷcəbəxʷ ʔə tiʔiɬ c̓ix̌c̓ix̌.

---

⁵⁵At this point Mr. Sam misspoke. What he intended to say is given here. What he actually said (and, of course what is heard on the tape) is lax̌dxʷ tiʔiɬ c̓ix̌c̓ix̌ which would mean *He remembered Fish Hawk.*

67. ʔuxʷtubəxʷ tiʔił sʔuladxʷ dxʷʔal tiʔił sčətxʷəd.

68. k̓ukʷcutyitəbəxʷ[56] ʔə tiʔəʔ c̓ix̌c̓ix̌ tiʔił syaʔyaʔs, sčətxʷəd.

69. hay q̓łaxʷ tiʔił sčətxʷəd.

70. huy dxʷcutəbəxʷ.

71. lax̌dxʷəxʷ tiʔił tushuy ʔə tiʔił c̓ix̌c̓ix̌.

72. ʔabači(ʔ)b tiʔəʔ sčətxʷəd ʔə tiʔəʔ łi[ʔ]łaʔx̌.

73. hədači(ʔ)bəxʷ.

74. 'c̓i·x̌əb, c̓ix̌əb, c̓ix̌əb, c̓ix̌əb.'

75. ʔi··.

76. xʷiʔəxʷ [k̓ʷi] gʷəsx̌ʷəs.

77. gʷəl bəcut,

78. 'c̓ix̌əb, c̓ix̌əb, c̓ix̌əb, c̓ix̌əb.'

79. bəhədači(ʔ)b.

80. xʷi·ʔ.

81. putəxʷ ləqʷup'qʷup'ači ʔə tiʔəʔ sčətxʷəd.

82. hay gʷəl ləbəč.

83. gʷəl [ʔu]gʷət'qʷad.

84. hay gʷəl təčtəbaxʷ tiʔəʔ sčətxʷəd ʔə tiʔəʔ c̓ix̌c̓ix̌.

85. bətədᶻiltubəxʷ.

86. hay, k̓ʷədatəbəxʷ tiʔəʔ łiʔłaʔx̌.

87. gʷəl cutəxʷ tiʔəʔ c̓ix̌c̓ix̌,

88. 'c̓i·x̌əb, c̓ix̌əb, c̓ix̌əb, c̓ix̌əb.'

89. hay gʷəl ləqa(h)il tiʔił sx̌ʷəs.

90. x̌ʷul'əxʷ ʔə(s)šuuc tiʔił ʔay'əds, sčətxʷəd.

91. pu·təxʷ ʔəsqʷup'qʷup'ači.

92. hay gʷəl łəgʷł.

93. hay, c̓əldub tiʔił sčətxʷəd ʔə tiʔəʔ c̓ix̌c̓ix̌.

---

[56]See footnote 52.

94. hay gʷəl haʔlicutəxʷ tiʔił sčətxʷəd ʔə tiʔił sɬəgʷəlyitəbs [(s)]ʔušəbitəbs ʔə tiʔił ċixčix̌ ʔə tiʔił sʔuladxʷ, ʔə tiʔił sx̌ʷəs.

95. gʷəl tulaʔyitəbəxʷ ʔə tiʔił sqʷʼiqʷʼəlałəd, saliʔ sqʷʼiqʷʼəlałəd.

96. huy gʷəl tux̌əcbidəxʷ.

97. gʷəl tuʔibibəš.

98. huyəxʷ tiʔił syəcəb.

99. dił shuys.

GLOSSARY

GLOSSARY

This glossary includes all words occurring in the four texts of this reader. However, it does not have all vocabulary used in the grammar section accompanying the reader.

The alphabetic order for Lushootseed is as follows: ʔ a b c cʼ č čʼ d dᶻ ə g gʷ h i ǰ k kʼ kʸ kʷ l lʼ ł ƛ (m) p pʼ q qʼ qʸ qʷ s š t tʼ u w wʼ xʷ x̌ x̌ʷ y yʼ.

Numbers after a gloss indicate the text and line number where the particular meaning is appropriate, while numbers in brackets, [ ], refer to a section in the grammar.

- ʔ -

ʔa·	Concluding syllable to a song. It has no lexical value. 2.52
ʔaʔild	See under ʔah.
ʔab	extend arm(s) / leg(s).
ʔabcut	extend self.
ʔabačiʔb	extend one's hand(s) 4.72.
ʔabšəd	take a step, extend leg.
ʔabgʷas	make several trips taking things somewhere.
ʔabuc(i)did	take lunch/dinner to someone.
ʔabaqəd	return something.
ʔabš	give something.
ʔabyi-	give.
ʔabalikʷ	give things away as in potlatching.
ʔac-	center of / middle of.
ʔacigʷəd	inside 1.38, 1.40.
sʔacus	face (See -us.)
ʔaciłtalbixʷ	Person, people; any indigenous person of the Americas.
ʔah	there, be there 2.13, 2.18, 2.55, 4.1, 4.35, 4.40, 4.50. łuʔa·(h) čəxʷ you will be there 3.52. ha·gʷəxʷ tiʔił sʔa··(h) ʔə tiʔił sbiaw Coyote was there for a long time 3.53. Be in existence 2.1, 4.65. łudəxʷʔa(h)s kʷi stab so

159

there would be something 2.17. ʔa·h gʷəl [a sentential adverb phrase 22.8] and there 2.21. x̌ʷuʔaʔild they would put it away 2.17.

ʔah	ʔah dəgʷi, siʔab dsyaʔyaʔ This is for you, my worthy friend 1.1.
ʔal	[As a preposition ʔal has many glosses in English such as] in, at, to, through, for, into, etc. [See 16.7a - 16.7b in the grammar.]
ʔalil	ʔaliləxʷ čəd tiʔəʔ sčətxʷəd Now I am considering Bear 2.5.
tulʔʔal	from 1.47.
ʔalʔal	house.
ʔaliləxʷ	See under ʔal.
ʔalqʷ	1. at the periphery, located away from the center 2. located at the back of an assembly hall (opposite of sula).
ʔalqʷ(ə)d	take something away from the fire, place something away from the center.
ʔalqʷbid	1. located away from the center in relation to some-one/something 2. located behind someone in a room.
ʔalš	cross-sex sibling, cross-sex cousin.
ʔalalš	plural of ʔalš.
ʔayʔəd	male friend of a man, a pal. (Sometimes used by a woman to refer to a friend of her same sex.)
ʔə	[oblique marker; genitive marker 12.2d]

Marking <u>agent</u>: 1.3, 1.11, 1.12, 1.29, 2.54, 3.36, 3.48, 4.46, 4.46, 4.51, 4.62, 4.66, 4.68, 4.83, 4.92.

Marking <u>patient</u>: 1.34, 1.42, 1.42, 2.20, 2.54, 3.43.

Marking <u>patient</u> of a -yi- verb: 3.8, 3.17, 4.21, 4.93, 4.93, 4.94.

Marking the *of*-relationship (See grammar 12.2d.): 1.2, 1.16, 1.27, 3.65.

Marking <u>agent</u> of a subordinate predicate (See grammar 21.2.): 1.31, 1.32, 1.44, 2.40, 2.40, 2.47, 3.3, 3.53, 4.71, 3.45.

Marking <u>patient</u> of a subordiante predicate (See grammar 21.2.): 4.20, 4.23.

Marking <u>subordinate</u> predicate: gʷəl tiʔił sʔuxʷ <u>ʔə tiʔił</u> sʔibəšs. *While going on his journey.* hikʷ ləcutukʷcut <u>ʔə tiʔił</u> sətəčs <u>ʔə tiʔił</u> sčalads tiʔił sbiaw. *[He] thumped loudly as he rolled [along] while he chased Coyote.*

about 2.1.

as 2.20, 3.30.

in 3.43, 3.47.

in/of 1.13, 1.38, 1.40.

in/on 4.49.

into 4.20.

onto 3.16.

over 4.72.

when/while 3.31.

while 3.30.

Unclassified: putəxʷ ləqʷup'qʷup'ači? ?ə ti?ə? sčətxʷəd. *Bear's hands shriveled right up.* 4.80.

?əɫəd	eat [This stem is agent oriented in spite of its appearance. Its patient oriented counterpart is ləkʷʷəd (or, in Skagit, huydxʷ).]
?əɫtxʷ	feed someone.
?i?ɫadəb	ləcu?i?ɫadəb ?ə ti?ə? sqʷʷəlaɫəd ?ə ti?iɫ X̌usqʷʷəls. *He was eating the berries as they ripened.* 2.20.
s?əɫəd	food.
?əX̌'	come.
?əX̌'c	come after something/someone; come for a specific purpose.
?əX̌'txʷ	bring someone/something.
?əpus	aunt, sister of one's father or mother.
?əs-	[Common variant of as-, the stative prefix, 10.3, 11.3].
?əxʷ-	[Combination of the prefixes ?əs- and dxʷ-].
?əx̌id	what? What is the matter?
dəxʷ?əx̌id-	why?
?əx̌ix̌txʷ	do something, do anything.
?u?əx̌ix̌ədəxʷ čəxʷ	What are you doing?
?əy'-	
?əy'dxʷ	find someone/something.
?i	and.

ʔi	an exclamation expressing *greatly, vastly* (4.37, 4.75).
ʔiʔab	wealth.
ʔiʔabil	become wealthy.
siʔab	nobleman, person of influence, leader.
siʔiʔab	high ranking people 2.30.
ʔiʔɬadəb	See under ʔəɬəd.
ʔibəš	walk, travel/journey by land (as opposed to travel by canoe).
ʔibəštxʷ	take someone for a walk, walk someone somewhere.
ʔibʔibəš	walk all about, travel a lot; many people walk.
ʔibibəš	pace back and forth, walk without achieving (or often even having) a destination.
ʔil-	ʔilgʷiɬ shoreline, shore, beach, bank.
ʔitut	sleep, x̌ʷalitut snore, sqəlalitut spirit power, dream.
ʔitutdubut	oversleep.
ʔəxʷʔitutəb	sleepy.
ʔiišəd	relative, friend, one's own people.
ʔu	[interrogative particel 2.3].
ʔu	Hey! 1.18. OK. 1.21. Oh. 1.26, 3.7, 3.67.
ʔu-	[Common variant of -u-, the perfective prefix 10.5, 11.3].
sʔuladxʷ	salmon and steelhead trout; (sometimes, 'fish' in a general sense).
ʔulal	bulrush, cattail.
ʔuləx̌	obtain from nature, gather, take and keep what one comes upon. (agent oriented).
ʔuləx̌əd	same as above except for being patient oriented.
ʔuləx̌yid	get (from nature) for someone.
ʔuluɬ	travel in a canoe, go by water (as opposed to walking, traveling over land).
-ʔulus	dxʷʔulus persistent person, a steady worker.
ʔusil	dive.
ʔusis	dive after something.
ʔušəb	pity, feel compassion.

ʔušəbid	pity someone.
[s]ušəbitəbs	out of pity for him 4.93.
ʔux̌ʷ	go.
ʔux̌ʷc	go after someone/something, go somewhere for a specific purpose.
ʔux̌ʷtx̌ʷ	take someone/something somewhere.

- a -

-aʔk̓ʷ-bix̌ʷ	group (viewed distributively).
-abac	body, bulky object.
-ač	head, crest. Compare sx̌əy'us, -qid, -us.
-ači?	hand, lower arm. Compare čaləs.
ad-	your [12.3, 12.3d, 12.4], you [20.3a].
-ad	I, me [first person singular clitic 14.4 - 14.4b].
-adx̌ʷ	variant of -əladx̌ʷ year [3.6].
-ag̓ʷ-	a derivational suffix by means of which various types of radical stems are converted to -il agent oriented stems, e.g. t̓ag̓ʷt *placed on top* becomes t̓ag̓ʷtag̓ʷil *climb(s) on top*.
-ag̓ʷəl	[reciprocal 9.7].
-ah- / -ap	buttocks, bottom, base.
-al-adi?	side of head.
-alc	Agent oriented suffix which denotes the manipulation or construction of something [7.3].
-aləp	you (plural) [second person plural clitic 14.4 - 14.4b].
-alik̓ʷ	agent oriented suffix with iterative meaning [7.3].
-ałi	we, us [first person plural clitic 14.4 - 14.5].
-ap / -ah-	buttocks, bottom, base.
as-	stative prefix [10.3, 11.3] most often pronounced as ʔəs-.
-as	[third person clitic 14.4 - 14.4b].

-axʷ	you (singular) [second person singular clitic 14.4 - 14.4b].
-axʷ	aspectual clitic [14.2 - 14.3c].
-ax̌ad	edge, at the side of.

- b -

-b	agent suffix [Lesson Three, 7.3].
-b	second member in suffix sequences [6.2] providing for an oblique complement [16.4. 16.5].
sbadil	mountain.
bap(a)	
ʔəsbap	busy.
bapad	pester / annoy someone.
bə-	again, anew, once more; additional [additive 13.6].
bəč(a)	
bəč	fall from a standing position.
ʔəsbəč	lies.
ʔəsbəčtxʷ	have someone/something laid out.
bəčad	set something down.
bəčaš	(equivalent to bəčad, [22.1b]).
bəčdxʷ	knock someone down / knock something over.
bəčagʷil	lie down.
bəčalikʷ	bet, wager.
dxʷbəčəb	sink.
dxʷbəčəbəd	sink something.
bəkʷ	be included; all.
bəkʷəd	take everything.
bəkʷdxʷ	manage to get all of something; xʷiʔ kʷi gʷəsbəkʷdxʷs *He couldn't manage [to eat] it all.*
bəkʷil	all finished, all gone, all used up.
bəkʷildxʷ	use something all up, finish something off.
bəkʷaʔkʷbixʷ	everyone.
bəɫ	full (container), full (of food or drink).

bəq'
    bəq'əd   put something in one's (own) mouth; swallow something.
    bəq'atxʷ   put something into someone else's mouth.

bəščəb   mink.
    bibščəb   young mink; a 'pet' way of referring to Mink.

bəsad   grow dark (night).

bəsqʷ   crab.

-bi-   secondary stem suffix which provides for the addition of the patient suffix **-d/-t-** to stems that otherwise could not take a patient ending at all (or could not take **-d/-t-** as a second patient suffix).

biac   meat.

sbiaw   coyote.

bibščəb   See under **bəščəb**.

-bi-d   locative and comparative suffix

- c -

-c   [a suffix marking patient oriented verbs, 4.3, 4.4, 5.4, 6.1].

-c   me [9.3b].

-c-əb   [a suffix marking patient oriented verbs, 8.3 - 8.3c].

cəxʷ-   [the combination of **d-** and **dəxʷ-**, 20.3] **cəxʷyaw'** that I should 3.21.

-cid   you [9.3b].

cil(i-)
    (ʔəs)cil   be protected/supported, be served (e.g., food). **ciliw'** basin, pan. **cicəl'šaad, dəxʷcicəl'šaadəb** something to walk on, carpet.
    cilid   support something, place something in/on a receptacle, dish [food] up.
    cilyid   dish [food] up for someone.
    (ʔəs)ciltxʷ   have [something/someone] put on/in a support or container.

ckʷaqid	always [predicate adverb 17.2].
cut	speak, say. This is the most all encompassing word in Lushootseed for human vocal utterances. **huy cutəxʷ** Then she sang 2.33. **cutəxʷ** chanted / spoke an incantation 4.87.
cut(t)əb	speak to someone (about something).
cuuc	tell someone (something).
ʔəxʷcutəb	thought so (all along) 3.41, 3.61, 3.73, 3.78; thought 4.53.
dxʷcutəbəxʷ	Then he thought (about it) 4.70.
gʷəxʷcutəb	might think 3.63.

- c' -

sc'aliʔ	heart.
c'əl-	win, pervail.
c'əlalikʷ	win (agent oriented) ... **łuc'əlalikʷ** ... (who) would win 2.31.
c'əld	defeat someone (patient oriented).
c'əldxʷ	manage to defeat someone (patient oriented).
c'ib	dip into; lick.
c'iẋ-	
c'iẋc'iẋ	fish hawk, osprey.
c'iẋəb	incantation Fish Hawk says in order to get fat to drip out from between his fingers to use as a dip for eating dried salmon.
c'ud	weak.
c'ukʷəb	flesh.

- č -

čaʔkʷ	seaward, in the direction of any body of water; at sea, out in the water (opposite of **t'aq't**).
dxʷčaʔkʷ	seaward, toward the water.
ladxʷčaʔkʷ	going toward the water (synonym of **kʷit'**), going further out to sea.

čaʔkʷtxʷ	take someone/something down to the water or out to sea.
čaʔkʷdxʷ	manage to get something/someone down to the water or out to sea.
čagʷəd	1. equivalent to the (more usual) čaʔkʷtxʷ. 2. fig., force someone to do something he does not want to do.
čagʷcut	go out from shore.
čagʷəb	be out at sea, be in the lake/river.
čagʷil	get too far out.
čagʷildxʷ	pick on someone, get the better of someone because he is out numbered or cornered.
čaʔkʷbid	(also pronounced čəʔkʷbid) located on the water side of something.
čad	where.
čal	how? in what condition or state?
čal(a)	chase, pursue; overtake; catch.
čalad	chase someone/something.
čaldxʷ	catch up with someone.
čaltxʷ	catch someone.
čaləs	hand, lower arm and hand. Compare -ačiʔ.
čcil	See under (x̌i)čəc.
čəbaʔ-əd	carry something/someone on one's back, backpack something / someone.
čəbid	Douglas fir. sčəbid bark (especially the bark of the Douglas fir tree which was the bark par excellence for the Lushootseed people).
čəbidac	Douglas fir tree.
-čəc	x̌ičəc red, red. x̌ičičc (a) penny.
čcil	become red.
čcild	redden something, make something red.
ʔəxʷčciligʷəd	red inside.
dxʷčacəb	red river (e.g., one flowing through iron rich land).
čəd	I [Lesson Two], me [4.5].
čəda	and I, and me [21.6b].

čəɫ	we [Lesson Two], us [4.5].
čɫa	and we [21.6b].
sčətxʷəd	(black) bear.
čəxʷ	you (singular) [Lesson Two, 4.5].
čxʷa	and you [21.6b].
čələp	you (plural) [Lesson Two, 4.5].
čələpa	and you [21.6b].
čɫa	See under čəɫ.
čubə	go up from shore, go up inland away from the water (opposite of kʷit', synonym of lədxʷt'aq't).
čubaac	go up from shore after something/someone.
čubəstxʷ	The old way of saying čubətxʷ [4.7d].
čubətxʷ	take someone/something up from shore.
-čup	cooking fire, campfire; firewood.
čxʷa	See under čəxʷ.
čxʷəluʔ	whale.

- č' -

č'aʔ-	dig, dig out, loosen ground for planting.
č'aʔəd	dig something up, dig it out (patient oriented stem)
č'aʔəb	dig something up (agent oriented stem).
č'aʔalikʷ	dig for edible roots and the like (agent oriented stem).
č'ač'as	1. child, youngster. 2. young.
č'aač'as	mature acting child.
ʔiɫč'ač'as	younger.
ʔixʷč'ač'as	young spouse.
č'awəyʔ	seashell (of any type). č'awəyʔulč ceramic dish. (See ɫaʔx̌.)
č'it	near (opposite of lil).
č'itcut	come close, approach.
č'itil	draw near.
č'itis	approach someone/something.

čʼitbid	located on the near side of something/someone.
čʼƛ̓aʔ	rock, stone. (In the third text of this reader, *boulder* would be the best gloss.)

- d -

d-	my [12.3, 12.3d, 12.4], I (me) [20.3a].
-d / -t-	a patient suffix [Lesson Three, 6.1].
daʔ(a)	name, call. **sdaʔ** name, **həlaʔb sdaʔs** is his real name (4.4).
daʔad	name someone.
daʔacutbid	tell someone one's (own) name.
dadatut	morning, (often pronounced as thought spelled **dadatu**).
dayʼ	only, uniquely, especially, completely [predicate adverb 17.2] after a while 4.42, **diɬ** [tiʔiɬ s]**dayʼ**]s . . . That was all.
dəčʼuʔ	one.
dəgʷ-	See under **dəkʷ**.
dəgʷi	you (singular), you are the one [19.3, 19.4].
dəkʷ	located inside something relatively small and confining.
dəgʷad	put something inside something relatively small.
dəgʷaš	(equivalent to **dəgʷad**).
dəgʷabacil	be inside the body of (a whale 1.13).
dəgʷagʷil	get inside something relatively small and confining.
dəxʷ-	where, when, reason why, method by which [Lesson Twenty].
sdəxʷiɬ	hunting canoe. This canoe is light weight and usually holds two hunters.
sdiʔdəxʷiɬ	small hunting canoe.
diɬ	the one(s) mentioned before, the one(s) about to be mentioned, that (which) he, she, it, they [19.4, 19.7, 22.9]. **diɬ** is most frequently used as a one word predicate. As such, one would expect a demonstrative [15.1 *ff.*] to introduce the following embedded sentence which serves as the complement of the **diɬ** predicate. However, all speakers

omit this demonstrative sometimes, and some usually do. In the first four texts of this reader the expected demonstrative is always lacking.

ds-	a sequence of prefixes **d-** + **s-**.
dsu-	a sequence of prefixes **d-** + **s-** + (ʔ)**u-**.
-du-	variant of **-dxʷ** [6.1, 9.1, 9.3a].
dukʷ	change, transform.
dukʷəladxʷ	next year, [Wait until] next year 2.39, 2.46.
dukʷibəɬ	the Changer, Transformer.
dxʷ-	to, toward.
dxʷʔal	to, toward, until; to 4.42, 4.63, 4.67; across [the entrance to] 3.49.
dxʷčaʔkʷ	seaward.
dxʷšəq	upward 4.11.
dxʷtəyil	travel upstream(ward).
dxʷtʼaqʼt	... **dxʷtʼaqʼt tiʔiɬ sɬalil** ... way up on shore 1.31.
dxʷ-	1. A derivational prefix which marks the stem as serving to contain, to hold within. 2. A secondary meaning of this **dxʷ-** designates a proclivity, what one has 'inside': **dxʷʔulus** a persistent person, a steady worker. 3. Also carrying this prefix are a number of stems referring to matters of the mind, the x̌əč: **dxʷcutəb** he thought 4.70,
dxʷx̌ʷalʼigʷəd	he gave up 4.24, 4.38.
-dxʷ / -du-	patient suffix expressing lack of full control on the part of an agent [5.1-5.4, 6.1, 9.1, 9.3a].

- dᶻ -

dᶻal-	turn around 180 degrees, turn over, go to the opposite side of something.
dᶻalq-	turn around, **dᶻalqʷus** look over one's own shoulder (lit. turn face around).
dᶻəlqcut	turn self around.

dᶻəlax̌adbid	visit someone.
dᶻəgʷaʔ	a great one for [doing something], well known for, famous for, professional.
dᶻəkʷ	1. wander. 2. be unstable.
ʔəsdᶻəkʷ	emotionally unstable person.
dᶻəkʷud	mislead someone, transgress.
dᶻəkʷadad	wrongdoing, sin.
dᶻəkʷaluʔ	driftwood and other debris.
dᶻəkʷdᶻəkʷ	wander about.
dᶻəkʷəkʷ	[The wind] keeps changing directions.
dᶻəl-	See under **dᶻal**.
dᶻub(u)	kick.
dᶻubud	kick someone/something.
dᶻubalikʷ	dance.

- ə -

-əč	See under **-ač**.
-əd	See under **-ad**.
-əladxʷ	year Cf. **sʔuladxʷ** salmon [3.6].
-ələp	See under **-aləp**.
əlgʷəʔ	By means of this word speakers make explicit that a third person referent is plural whether as agent, patient or possessor, e.g., *they, them, their(s)*. It is always optional; pragmatic considerations determine its use -- not grammar. Following a vowel or when syllable initial, it is spelled (and pronounced) **həlgʷəʔ** [12.6].
-əɬi	See under **-aɬi**.
-əs	See under **-as**.
əw'ə	A predicate particle [17.1 - 17.1c] expressing mild surprise. Following a vowel, it is spelled (and pronounced) **haw'ə(ʔ)**.

-əxʷ	variant of **-axʷ** *you* [14.4 - 14.4b].
-əxʷ	variant of the aspectual clitic **-axʷ** [14.2 - 14.3c].

- g -

gədu	bum, no good so-and-so.
gəlgəb	mumble.
gəlkʼ	wind around, entangle.
gəlkʼəd	wind something (such as string) around [something].
gəlkʼalikʷ	knit.
gət	guy, fellow.

- gʷ -

gʷ-	[subjunctive prefix 12.2b, 13.1, 13.4, 14.4b].
gʷə-	variant of **gʷ-** occurring before consonants.
sgʷaʔ	one's own [22.7].
gʷaadgʷad	talk, converse, get to talking, express an opinion.
gʷadadgʷad	talk over, discuss 1.22, 2.31; converse 4.52.
-gʷas	pair.
gʷat	who, whom [19.4 - 19.6b].
gʷax̌ʷ	two or more people (go for a) walk.
gʷax̌ʷtxʷ	cause someone to walk with one.
gʷə-	See under **gʷ-**.
gʷəčʼ-	
gʷəčʼəd	look for something/someone (patient oriented stem).
gʷəčʼəb	someone seeks something/someone (agent oriented stem).
gʷəčʼalikʷ	someone regularly seeks something/someone (agent oriented).
gʷədəxʷ-	sequence of **gʷ-** + **dəxʷ-**.
gʷədəxʷu-	sequence of **gʷ-** + **dəxʷ-** + **(ʔ)u-**.

gʷəl	and, or, but [sentential adverb 22.8 - 22.8b].
gʷəs-	sequence of **gʷ**- + **s**-.
gʷəsu-	sequence of **gʷ**- + **s**- + (ʔ)**u**-.
gʷət'qʷad	See under -**t'qʔ'ʷ(u)**-.
-gʷił	canoe, waterway, curved side, narrow passageway.
gʷu-	Sequence of **gʷ**- + (ʔ)**u**-.

- h -

haʔkʷ	for a long time; ago. all along 3.41, 3.61, 3.73, 3.78 [17.2].
hagʷ-	for a long time 1.38, 1.40, 3.52.
haʔł	good, nice; pretty, handsome.
haʔləb	calm weather, good weather.
haʔłil	weather turns nice, [something] becomes good.
haʔlid	make [something] nice, clean [something], clear it up.
haʔlicut	situated comfortably 4.94.
dəxʷ(h)aʔłs	that was any good 3.18, 3.31.
hay	next [sentential adverb 22.8, 22.8a].
haydxʷ	know.
heʔehe	Concluding syllables in a song. They have no lexical value. 2.52
həd	warm, hot.
pədhədəb	summer.
(həd)hədačiʔb	warm one's hands.
hədil	weather becomes warm.
hədqʷəb	something is warm.
hədqʷəbid	warm/heat something.
həd'ʔiw'	be inside / enter a house. Ususally pronounced as if spelled **hədiw'**.
həd'ʔiw'b	This form is often equivalent to **həd'ʔiw'**. [See 4.6].
həd'ʔiw'txʷ	take/bring someone inside [See 4.6.].
həd'ʔiw'd	take/bring someone inside [See 4.6.].

həd'iw'dubut	get one's self inside [the cave] 3.48.
həd'iw'c	go/come in after someone/something [See 4.6.].
həla'b	really, a lot, real [predicate adverb 17.2 - 17.3 (Speakers sometimes also use həla'b as a modifier in complements.)] c'ix̌c'ix̌ ti'ił həla'b sda's *Fish Hawk is his real name* 4.4.
həli'	live, be alive.
səli'	soul.
həli'tx^w	cure someone, allow someone to live.
həli'dx^w	help someone live, give life to someone.
həli'dubut	recover (esp., recover one's soul).
həli'il	heal, become well.
həli'is	... stab k^wi g^wədəx^w(h)əli'iss əlg^wə' ... whatever they could live on 2.15.
hig^wil	See under hik^w.
hiił	happy, glad.
hik^w	big.
hig^wəd	support someone, uphold.
hiktx^w	respect someone.
hig^wil	become big, become important / influential.
hik^wbid	bigger.
hud	fire, firewood.
hudud	burn something, heat something up, turn on a light. (Compare ləx̌əd.)
hud(d)x^w	manage to burn something (such as wet wood); inadvertently set something on fire.
'əshudtx^w	keep fire going.
hudčup	build a fire.
x^w(h)udad	ashes.
huy	finish(ed), complete(d) 1.51, 1.52, 3.80, 4.39, 4.98. dił shuys *That's the end* 2.66, 4.99. stabəx^w k^wi łushuys ... *What are they going to do?* 3.59. stab ti'ił suhuyləp *What are you folks doing?* 3.6.

huyud	make / prepare / do something. **ɫuhuyutəbəxʷ čʼit tiʔiɫ dəxʷʔibəš čəɫ** *where we are going will be made near* (i.e., *our trip will be short*) 3.10.
huydxʷ	manage to do something, figure something out, solve a problem
huytxʷ	cause to be a certain way, make a certain way. fire someone from employment.
huyil	become.
huyalc	build / construct / complete something.
huyalikʷ	create.
huy	then, next [sentential adverb 22.8, 22.8a].

- i -

-igʷəd	inside human/animal body; inside small, tight enclosure.
-igʷs	things, possessions. **stabigʷs** prised possessions 3.15 [See 16.10.]
-il	[A suffix marking agent oriented verbs. See Lesson Four.]
-il	[Common suffix on experiencer stems, 4.2 - 4.2b].
-is	[A suffix marking patient oriented verbs built upon **-il**, (i.e., **-il** + **-s** > **-is**) 4.1].

- ǰ -

ǰəsəd	foot, lower leg, foot and shank.
ǰiqʼ	soak, drown.
ǰiqʼid	immerse something.
ǰiqʼcut	soak self.
ǰiqʼagʷil	enter the water.
ʔəsǰiqʼtxʷ	have something immersed.
ǰiqʼaladʸəd	set fishing nets.
ǰuʔil	enjoy one's self, have a good time.

- k -

kay'kay'	Stellar's jay.
skəyu	corpse, ghost.
skəyuil	become like a ghost / become a corpse.
skəyuhali	place where the dead are place, graveyard.
kiis	stand up.
kiistxʷ	stand someone/something up.
kiisbid	stand beside someone/something.
(ʔəs)kisəč	bird's crest, hackles of a dog, hair stands on end.

- k' -

k'aʔk'aʔ	crow.
k'adəyuʔ	rat.
k'awdxʷ	bump into someone/something, touch someone/something.
k'iɬ(i)	hang on a peg/nail/corner of a door/ etc.
k'iɬid	hang something on a peg/nail/etc.

- kʷ -

kʷaʔ	however, although; naturally, as is known [predicate particle 17.1a].
kʷatač	climb up. **kʷatajəxʷ** climb(s) up now.
kʷatačaac	climb after someone/something.
kʷaxʷ(a)	help.
kʷaxʷad	help someone.
kʷaxʷdxʷ	manage to help someone, able to help someone.
kʷaxʷadad	spiritual help.
kʷiʔkʷxʷad	a little helper.
kʷxʷad	good luck.
kʷəd(a)	get, take; hold, grasp.

kʷəd	have a spell/seizure.
kʷədad	take 4.29, take [the other one] 4.31, was taken 4.86.
kʷəd(d)xʷ	manage to get, manage to grasp.
kʷədalikʷ	take again and again (as in fishing, for example).
kʷədaʔ	might, maybe [predicate particle 17.1a, 17.3b].
kʷədiʔ	way over there (far out of sight), long, long ago [adverbial demonstrative 15.4].
kʷi	[adjectival demonstrative referring to hypothetical and/or remote entities 15.2].
skʷiʔxʷ	rhizomes of the braken fern.
kʷixʷ(i)	kʷixʷid sound of pounding, the ringing sound one makes as his adze strikes a log being carved into a canoe.
kʷukʷcut	cook [a loan word from English equivalent to qʷʷəl-].

- kʷ -

kʷatʼaq	a large cattail mat used most often to line the inside walls of houses. These mats were also used to make temporary shelters during the summer.
kʷʷəɬ	hearsay, "... they say." [predicate particle 17.1, 17.1a].
kʷʷəɬ	spill, pour.
kʷʷəɬəd	pour something.
kʷʷəɬdxʷ	spill something.
ʔəskʷʷəɬtxʷ	have something poured out / emptied onto.
kʷʷɬalikʷ	serve liquid repeatedly (e.g., to all the guests).
kʷʷɬibəd	container made from thinly woven cedar bark strips.
kʷʷɬičəd	spill on / pour on someone/something.
kʷʷikʷʷəɬ	trickle down.
kʷʷəɬkʷʷɬad	keep pouring something.
kʷʷil	peek, look from behind something.
kʷʷilid	peek at someone/something; look in on someone but not stay to visit.
kʷʷildxʷ	manage to get a peek.

kʷiltxʷ   use something to peek (at someone/something).
kʷilil   peer.

kʷit'   go down to the water's edge (opposite of čubə, synonym of
                                lədxʷča'kʷ).

'əskʷit'algʷił   be down on the shore.
kʷit'txʷ   take someone/something down to the water's edge.
kʷit'txʷyid   take [something] down to the water's edge for someone.
'iłkʷit'txʷ   take one of two down to the water's edge.

skʷuy   mother
kʷuyə'   mom, mother (in addressing her).
ciłbəskʷuy   half-sibling with mother in common.

- l -

la'   point out, establish the location of something.
la'əd   point something out.
la'cut   introduce self.
la'yid   show someone where [something] is located.
'əsla'txʷ   know where something is located.
'əbsla'il   have a location.

lax̌   remember.
laxdxʷ   remember someone/something.
laxc   reminisce about people/events.
laxtxʷ   remind someone.
laxbid   remember the whole affair.

lə-   [progressive prefix 11.3b - 11.6].

ləcu-   [continuous prefix 11.3b, 11.8 - 11.8c].

ləgʷəb   youth, young man.

ləkʷəd   eat something, put something into the mouth (patient oriented
                                verb). Compare 'əłəd.

ləkʷdxʷ   manage to eat something / to get something into the mouth.
ləkʷyid   eat someone else's food.
ləkʷucidid   kiss someone.

ləs-	[progressive state 11.3b, 11.7 - 11.7b].
ləx̌	light.
ləx̌əd	light something up (Compare **hudud** turn on a light.)
ləx̌il	grow light. **sləx̌il** day.
liʔluʔ	See under **luʔ**.
lił-	by way of, by a particular route [See 16.7a.]
luʔ	hole in (but not through) something (Compare **tʼuʔ** a hole through something.) **səsluʔ** a cave 3.49.
ʔəsliʔluʔ	a small hole in the ground, a small cave 3.46.
luʔud	bore a hole.
luʔucut	spawn (lit. *make holes for themselves*).
luh-	hear, listen.
luud	hear something/someone.
luutəb	be overheard.
ludx̌ʷ	happen to hear about something.
luuc	listen to someone/something.
lux̌ʼ	old. old person.
lux̌ʼlux̌ʼ	elders, ancestors.
lux̌ʼəb	be old.
lux̌ʼil	grow old.
lux̌ʼbid	older than someone/something.
ʔiłlux̌ʼ	older, the eldest.
luud	See under **luh-**.

- ł -

łaʔx̌	bowl, platter (Compare **qʷłəyʔulč** large wooden bowl, **čʼawəyʔulč** ceramic dish, **ciliwʼ** basin, pan.)
łiʔłaʔx̌	small bowl, small platter.
łačʼ	fire goes out.
łačʼad	put fire out.
łačʼdxʷ	manage to put fire out.
łačʼalikʷ	fight forest fire. **dxʷsłačʼalikʷ** fireman, firefighter.

sɫadəyʔ	woman.
sɫaaɫədəyʔ	girls.
sɫadadəyʔ	woman (living) alone.
sɫaɫdəyʔ	girl.
sɫaɫədəyʔ	girl friend.
sɫəɫadəyʔ	women.
ɫalil	go ashore, land/dock a boat; reach the end of a row when harvesting crops.
ɫalis	go ashore after something.
ɫaliltxʷ	put ashore, take to shore.
ɫalildxʷ	manage to reach shore.
ɫaɫlil	dwell, live some place. dəxʷəsɫaɫlils where he dwelled 4.1.
ɫax̌	dark(ness).
ɫax̌il	grow dark. sɫax̌il night. səɫax̌il evening.
ɫəč	"get started" under influence of one's spirit power.
ɫčil	arrive, ɫiɫčil arrive occasionally.
ɫčis	arrive for someone/something, arrive for a specific purpose.
ɫčisič	be visited at an inconvenient time.
ɫčiltxʷ	arrive with someone/something.
ɫčildxʷ	manage to arrive with someone/something.
ɫčiltxʷyitəb	something/someone is brought for the benefit of someone.
ɫəgʷɫ	leave.
ɫəgʷəlb	be left by someone.
ɫəgʷəldxʷ	inadvertently leave someone behind.
ɫəgʷəlyid	leave someone/something for someone, ... ʔə tiʔiɫ sɫəgʷəlyitəbs [(s)]ušəbitəbs ʔə tiʔiɫ c'ix̌c'ix̌ ʔə tiʔiɫ sʔuladxʷ ... with the salmon which Fish Hawk, [out of] pity left for him ... 4.94.
ɫət'əd	flip something away.
ɫi	[second person (12.4) plural imperative 11.10].
ɫiʔɫaʔx̌	See under ɫaʔx̌.
ɫiʔɫdahəb	See under ɫid.
ɫič'	get cut. səxʷɫič'(aʔkʷčup) a saw. ɫič'tadəd scar.

ɬičʼid	cut someone/something, **ɬiɬičʼ** cut into little pieces, **ɬičʼličʼgʷasəd** slice something, **ɬičʼšadid** amputate someone's leg/foot.
ɬičʼib	cut cattails for mat making; cut grass, etc. to make something.
ɬičʼdxʷ	accidentally cut someone/something.
ɬid	tied. **sɬidalšəd** tumpline (named for the way it is made using the foot). **dxʷɬidič** bowstring.
ɬidap	trawl. **ɬiʔɬdahəb** troll (for fish).
ɬidid	tie someone/something.
ɬidgʷasəd	tie them together (to make [rope]) longer.
ɬixʷ	three.
ɬixʷəɬdat	three days.
ɬu-	[irrealis prefix 13.1, 13.3, 13.4, also 9.2].
ɬ(u)ads-	sequence of **ɬu-** + **ad-** + **s-**.
ɬubə-	sequence of **ɬu-** + **bə-**.
ɬudəxʷ-	sequence of **ɬu-** + **dəxʷ-**.
ɬuds-	sequence of **ɬu-** + **d-** + **s-**.
ɬuqʼʷ(u)	peel.
ɬuqʼʷud	peel something.
ɬuqʼʷač	bald head.
ɬus-	sequence of **ɬu-** + **s-**.

- x̌ʼ -

x̌ʼacʼ(a)-	cinch.
x̌ʼacʼad	cinch something [unattested].
x̌ʼacʼəb	cinch up (one's own belt).
x̌ʼacʼahəb	cinch up at one's own waist.
x̌ʼacʼapəd	belt.
x̌ʼax̌ʼacʼapəd	ant [lit. *little cinched up [one]*].
x̌ʼal	put on clothing.
x̌ʼalš	put something on.

x̣ʼalib	[See 22.1.c.]
x̣ʼaldxʷ	manage to get something on, e.g., struggle to put on something a bit too tight.
ʔəsx̣ʼaltxʷ	wear something.
x̣ʼalyid	put article of clothing on someone.
x̣ʼalabacəb	clothe body. sx̣ʼalabac garment, clothing.
x̣ʼalalicʼaʔb	put clothes on. x̣ʼalalicʼaʔ clothes.
x̣ʼalšədəb	put shoe(s) on. sx̣ʼalšəd skis, snowshoes.
x̣ʼalšədid	put shoe(s) on someone.
x̣ʼalšədyid	put shoe(s) on someone for someone else (as in helping a busy mother dress a child).
x̣ʼalaliqʷəb	put on a hat.
x̣ʼalʼ	also, too [predicate adverb 17.2].
sx̣ʼəlayʔ	shovel-nose canoe (used on rivers. It was poled, not paddled.)
x̣ʼiq(i)-	emerge.
x̣ʼiq	emerge, come out of hiding, emerge from thick brush, come out of the water.
x̣ʼiqid	take something/someone out of enclosure.
x̣ʼiqdxʷ	manage to get someone/something our of an enclosure.
x̣ʼiqagʷil	come out of an enclosure.
x̣ʼqil	come out of hibernation.
x̣ʼu-	[habitual prefix 13.1, 13.2].
x̣ʼ(u)as-	sequence of x̣ʼu- + as- / əs-.
x̣ʼub	well, fine, good, OK.
x̣ʼubəd	agree to something.
x̣ʼubtxʷ	get something fixed / arranged satisfactorily.
x̣ʼubil	become well.
x̣ʼubildxʷ	agree with someone.
x̣ʼub	[as predicate adverb 17.2, 17.2a] should, ought to, had better.
x̣ʼubə-	sequence of x̣ʼu- + bə-.
x̣ʼubəxʷ-	sequence of x̣ʼu- + bə- + as-/əs- + dxʷ-.
x̣ʼudəxʷ-	sequence of x̣ʼu- + dəxʷ-.
x̣ʼuil	thin person.
x̣ʼux̣ʼuil	very thin.

ƛ̕us-	sequence of ƛ̕u- + s-.
ƛ̕x̌ʷay̓	dog salmon, chum.
pədƛ̕x̌ʷay̓	autumn, November, dog salmon time.

- m -

mi̓man̓	small, ʔəsmi̓man̓ It [must] be small. 3.43.

- p -

pač(a)	lay out gifts, display gifts to be given.
pak̓ʷahəb	lie with rear up.
pəd-	time of.
pišpiš	domestic cat. pipšpiš kitten.
pus	get hit by something thrown or falling (experiencer stem).
pusud	throw at someone/something, hit something/someone by throwing something (patient oriented stem).
pusdx̌ʷ	accidentally hit by throwing, manage to hit by throwing something.
pusil	throw, toss (agent oriented stem). dx̌ʷspusil baseball pitcher.
pupsil	toss pebbles.
pusilyid	pitch for someone.
pusildx̌ʷ	throw/toss something (instrumental oriented stem).
pusiltx̌ʷ	throw someone (as in wrestling) (patient oriented causative stem).
-pus-	
ʔəx̌ʷpusəb	raise one's head.
put	adverb [17.2a] which intensifies the significance of its predicate [16.1]: very 3.4, 3.55, just 4.81, 4.91, just plain 1.45, just plumb 2.22, 2.56, even more 2.43, still more 2.50, really! 2.48, 3.54, sound(ly) 2.57.

- p̓ -

p̓aƛ̓aƛ̓	junk 3.14, 3.32, worthless 3.17.
p̓ayəq	hew, especially hew out a canoe, (loosely: make a canoe), use an adze.
p̓il	flat.
p̓ilid	flatten something.
p̓iləb	something goes flat; be flooded.

- q -

sqa	older sibling, older cousin, dəxʷsqatəd older siblings, older cousins.
qa(h)	many, much, a lot.
qa(h)il	becomes a lot, ləqa(h)il there comes to be a lot (of).
qaw̓qs	raven.
qc̓ap	Kitsap, a famous leader of a Southern Lushootseed group.
qəladiʔ	up-rooted tree/stump, snag(s).
qiʔqəl̓adiʔ	the daughter of Basket Ogress (so named because her hair was so tangled).
sqəlalitut	spirit power, guardian spirit.
qəlb / qələb	rain. qəlbalqʷuʔ rain water.
qəlbič	get caught in the rain.
dxʷqəlb	A very common name for rivers and streams in Lushootseed territory. The name refers to the turbid quality of the water.
ʔəxʷqələbil	[A river] is turbid.
qəɫ, qɫ-	wake up; regain consciousness, come to.
qəɫəd	wake someone up.
qəɫdxʷ	inadvertently awaken someone.
qəsiʔ	uncle, brother of one's father or mother.
-qid	1. head (See sx̌əy̓us.) 2. dxʷ- . . . . -qid voice.

-iy-a-qid	1. top of some relatively large or high object. 2. over one's head.
-əl-qid	wool, hair.

- q' -

q'axʷ	freeze. **sq'axʷ** ice.
q'axʷad	freeze something.
q'c-	**q'cač** strike back of head (against something).
sq'əďzuʔ	(human) hair.
q'il	1. ride in canoe (or any conveyance). 2. (salmon) travel upstream.
q'ilid	load things (into canoe (or other conveyance).
q'iltxʷ	load canoe (or other conveyance).
q'ildxʷ	1. manage to load things. 2. manage to load canoe.
q'ilil	go along for the ride.
q'ilagʷil	get on board, mount a horse.
q'ilagʷis	catch a ride.
q'iləb	load one's own canoe.
q'ilad	the load carried.
q'il'bid	canoe (general term, includes all types).
q'ilicut	a riffle in a river, white water.
q'əwab	howl.

- qʷ -

sqʷaliʔ	hay.
sqʷiʔqʷaliʔ	hay, grass. **sqʷiʔqʷaliʔali** hayfield. **sqʷiqʷqʷaliʔ** grass of a lawn.
sqʷəbayʔ	dog. **sqʷi(ʔ)qʷəbayʔ** puppy.
qʷib	prepare, ready.

qʷibid	prepare something/someone, fix something; ... čəda łuqʷibid *and I will fix him!* 3.13 [This use of **qʷibid** is a loan translation from the English colloquial expression.]
ʔəsqʷibtxʷ	have something/someone ready, have it prepared.
qʷibil	recover health (emotional or physical).
qʷic	go downstream (opposite of **təyil**).
qʷicʼ	unwilling, indifferent, lazy.
qʷicʼbid	unable to do something.
qʷist	bovine.
qʷłayʔ	log, stick. Sometimes used to mean *tree* of any kind.
qʷłəyʔulč	large wooden bowl or platter (See **łaʔx̌**.)
qʷuʔ	water, especially fresh water as opposed to sea water.
qʷuʔqʷaʔ	drink.
qʷuʔqʷa(ʔ)did	drink something.
qʷu(ʔ)bid	(mouth) waters for something.

- qʷ̓ -

qʷ̓əl	ripe, ripen. **sqʷ̓əlałəd** berry (lit., *ripe food*). **sqʷ̓iqʷ̓əlałəd** little berry.
dxʷsqʷ̓əl	hot (weather).
dxʷsqʷ̓əlil	grow warm (weather).
qʷ̓əl(ə)d	cook something.
qʷ̓əl(ə)b	someone cooks.
qʷ̓uʔ	gather, unite.
(ʔ)əsqʷ̓uʔ	be gathered.
qʷ̓uʔəd	gathered something, collected something.
qʷ̓uʔtəb	[people] were brought together 1.47, 2.30, 4.28.
qʷ̓upʼ	shrivel, shrink. -**qʷ̓upʼqʷ̓upʼačiʔ** shrivel(ed) hands 4.81, 4.91.

- s -

s-	[a nominalizing prefix 3.2, 12.1, 18.1 *ff*, 20.1 *ff*]. If a noun cannot be found under s-, it is to be sought under the following consonant [3.2, 12.1].
-s	Third person suffix [12.3 - 12.3d, 12.4a, 12.5, 12.6, 20.3].
-s	Goal suffix [4.1, 4.4, 5.4].
saʔ	bad.
saʔtxʷ	dislike someone/something.
saʔil	become bad; get in trouble.
saʔsəliʔ	See under **saliʔ**.
saliʔ	two.
saliʔil	become two, become the second.
saʔsəliʔ	two small items.
səsaʔliʔ	two people.
saqʷ	fly.
saqʷtxʷ	fly off with something/someone.
saxʷəb	jump, run (especially in a short burst of energy as opposed to **təlawil** which is to run for a sustained period).
saxʷəbid	jump/run after something/someone.
saxʷəbtxʷ	run off with something/someone, kidnap someone.
siʔab	See under **ʔiʔab**.
siʔiʔab	See under **ʔiʔab**.
sixʷ	Predicate particle [17.1] meaning *again, as usual*. (Often - but by no means always - **sixʷ** carries connotations of mild annoyance.)
stab	what?, what (in the sense of an English relative pronoun) 2.54, thing 3.31. (Ultimately, this word is derived from **tab**.)
stabigʷs	belongings, (prized) possessions, treasure.
suʔsuqʷaʔ	See under **suqʷaʔ**.
sula	1. located at the center of a room 2. located at the front of an assembly hall (opposite of **ʔalqʷ**).
sulad	place something in the center of the room.

sulayid	place [something] directly in front of someone (especially, in front of someone who is facing the center of the room) for that person.
sulatxʷ	bring something toward the center of the room / the front of an assembly.
sulabid	1. located toward the center in relation to someone/something. 2. located toward the front of someone in a room.
suqʷ'a'	younger sibling, younger cousin.
su'suqʷ'a'	little younger sibling, little younger cousin.
suqʷ'suqʷ'a'	younger siblings, younger cousins.

- š -

-š	Suffix for patient oriented stems [22.1a - 22.1c].
šab	dry.
šabad	dry something.
šabəb	dry something of one's own, e.g., clothing, body part.
šabalikʷ	dry to preserve food.
šaw'	bone.
šəbad	enemy.
dxʷšəɬəb	See under šuɬ.
šəq	up in the air, high. **šqabac** on top of some relatively bulky object.
šəqəd	raise something.
šqil	hold in high regard.
dxʷšəq	upward.
liɬšəq	by way of the top, be on top.
tul'šəq	from above.
šəqbid	upper side of something, at the top.
šqabac	on top (Compare **t'agʷt.**)
šqabac	See under šəq.
šudxʷ	See under šuɬ.
šul(u)	pass beneath, sheathe, insert, enter cramped place.

šulud	put something beneath something, insert something into something.
šulagʷil	crawl beneath, crawl/slither/slide into cramped place 3.42.
šulagʷis	crawl beneath after something/someone.
šulagʷildubut	get self into cramped space 3.44.
šuɫ	see, look; appearance.
dxʷšəɫəb	look through water.
šudxʷ	see someone/something.
šudubut	able to see because view is not obstructed.
šuɫalbut	able to see because one's eyes are good/healthy.
šuɫtxʷ	show someone (something).
šuuc	look at something.
šuucbicut	look after one's self.
šuucbid	keep an eye out for someone/something, look for someone (to come by).
šuucəb	be visited, [someone comes to] see someone.
šuuc	See under **šuɫ**.

- t -

-t-	See under **-d**.
tab	As a verb stem **tab** is a proverb something like *do* in English. It designates an act that one knows about from context.
stab	See **stab** under **s**.
tagʷəxʷ	hungry.
talə	money [See 14.6b.]
taqʷuʔ	thirst, thirsty.
tə	[adjectival demonstrative 15.2].
təč	roll, **tədtəč** roll off, tumble down.
təǰəd	roll something, roll someone over 4.84.
tədʸil	go to bed, **ʔəstədʸil** lie in bed, be in bed 4.50.
tədʸiltxʷ	put someone to bed.
tədʸis	go to bed with someone, go to bed for a specific purpose.

təlawil   run (especially for a sustained period as opposed to **saxʷəb** which means to run with a short burst of energy). **titəlawil** jog.

   təlawiltxʷ   exercise an animal such as a horse; operate a machine.

   təlawis   run for a specific goal, run after something/someone.

tətyika   name of Young Mink's younger brother/ younger cousin.

təyil   go upstream (in a boat, by swimming, by walking along the bank) (Fish, humans and any animal can be said to **təyil**.) Opposite of **qʷic**.

ti   [adjectival demonstrative 15.2].

tiʔəʔ   this [adjectival demonstrative 15.2, 15.2f, 15.2g], this [pronominal demonstrative 15.3].

   tiʔiʔəʔ   these [15.2c].

   tsiʔəʔ   this [15.2, 15.2f, 15.2g].

tiʔiɬ   that [adjectival demonstrative 15.2, 15.2f, 15.2g], that [pronominal demonstrative 15.3].

   tiʔiʔiɬ   those [15.2c].

   tsiʔiɬ   that [15.2, 15.2f, 15.2g].

tiləb   immediately, right away; abruptly, suddenly, unexpectedly; right there, directly [predicate adverb 17.2, 17.2a], way (up) 1.31.

stiqíw   horse. **stitiqiw** pony, foal. **stiqtiqíw** horses.

tsiʔəʔ   See under **tiʔəʔ**.

tsiʔiɬ   See under **tiʔiɬ**.

tu-   [past 13.1, 13.5].

-tu-   See under **-txʷ**.

t(u)as-   sequence of **tu-** + **as-**.

stubš   man, male, (in appropriate contexts: son, boy).

   stuʔtəbš   a single man among many women.

   stububš   men.

   stutubš   boy.

   stuutubš   boys.

tud-   sequence of **tu-** + **d-**.

tudi^ʔ	over there, yonder [adverbial demonstrative 15.4].
tukʷʼud	thumping sound.
stuləkʷ	river.
tuľ-	from [16.7a].
tuľʔal	from [16.7a].
tus-	sequence of **tu-** + **s-**.
tux̌ʷ	merely, just; otherwise, or else, instead, in contrast to the usual, in contrast to the expected [predicate adverb 17.2].
-tx̌ʷ, -tu-	causative suffix for patient oriented stem [Lesson One, 5.4].

- t' -

t'agʷt	1. placed on top of something high (compare **šqabac**.) 2. noon.
t'at'gʷət	noon.
t'agʷtəd	put something on top of something (especially something high) [22.1b].
t'agʷtəš	put something on top of something (especially something high) [22.1b].
t'agʷagʷil	climb up onto the top of something.
t'aq't	located up inland away from the shore or river bank (opposite of **ča^ʔkʷ**).
dx̌ʷt'aq't	toward the land, toward the mountains away from the shore.
lədx̌ʷt'aq't	going toward land, going up inland (synonym of **čubə**).
t'aq'tbid	located on the inland side of something.
t'as(a)	pay.
t'asad	pay for something (patient oriented). **t'asatəb** something is paid for.
t'asyid	pay someone. **t'asyitəb** pay someone for something he bought for someone.
t'as(ə)bil	pay for something (agent oriented).
t'asəbildubut	pay one's bill.
t'əqʷ-	See under **t'qʷ(u)-**.

t'əs	cold (weather). **pədt'əs** winter.
t'əsəd	warm something next to open fire, bake something.
t'əsəb	cold weather.
t'sil	weather becomes cold.
t'ilib	sing.
t'ilibtxʷ	sing to someone; play a phonograph, turn on a radio, etc.
st'ilib	song.
t'isəd	arrow.
-t'qʷˀad	See under **t'qʷˀ(u)-**.
t'qʷˀ(u)-	break flexible object in two, snap in two.
t'əqʷˀgʷas	come apart.
t'əqʷˀtxʷ	stop a song.
t'qʷˀud	break something flexible in two.
gʷət'qʷˀad	faint, pass out. **ˀugʷət'qʷˀad** He passed out 4.60, 4.83.
t'uˀ	hole through something (Compare **luˀ** a hole in but not through something.)
ˀəst'uˀ	[The cloth] has a hole in it.
t'ukʷˀ	go/come home.
t'ukʷˀtxʷ	take/bring someone home.
t'ukʷˀc	go / come home for something

- u -

-u-	[perfective prefix 10.5, 11.3].
uˀxʷ	still, yet [predicate particle 17.1 - 17.1c].
-ubuł	us [9.3b].
-ubułəd	you folks [9.3b].
-uł	us [9.3a].
-ułəd	you folks [9.3a].
-us	face (See **sˀacus**.); head (See **sx̌əyˀus**, **-qid**, **-ač**.); upper part.

- w -

swatixʷtəd	land, region, place; country, world.
we	Syllable concluding a song which has no lexical value.
wəqʼəb	cedar chest, box (in general).
swətixʷtəd	trees and plants (in general).
wiliqʼʷ(i)	question, ask.
wiliqʼʷid	question someone, ask someone a question.
wiwʼsu	children.
swuqʷad(iʔ)	loon.

- xʷ -

xʷ-	[reduced from of dxʷ- 'contain'].
xʷakʷʷil	tired.
xʷakʷʷis	tired of something, especially tired of something because of the way it affects one.
xʷakʷʷilbid	tired of something, especially tired of something because of one's own internal emotional or physical state.
xʷakʷʷisbid	tired of someone for what that individual does, e.g., **ʔəsxʷakʷʷisbitəbəxʷ čəd ʔə tiʔəʔ ƛʼudsudᶻəlax̌ad** *[They] are tired of me habitually visiting.*
xʷeʔeʔ	Sequence of syllables ending a song which have no lexical value.
xʷəb	throw; discard; **xʷəbəbxʷəbaladi(ʔ)b** *toss head from side to side.*
xʷəbəd	throw someone down as in wrestling; throw something away.
xʷəbagʷil	throw self down.
xʷiʔ	no, not. [See Lesson Eighteen for a discussion of xʷiʔ.] **xʷiʔ kʷ[i gʷ]adsukʼawdxʷ** *Don't bump it.* 1.19. **xʷiʔ [kʷi] gʷədəxʷ(h)aʔɬs** *[It is] not good for anything.* 3.18. **xʷiʔ [kʷi] gʷəstab[s kʷi] dəxʷ(h)aʔɬs** *Nothing [given was] good for anything.* 3.31.

xʷiʔ kʷi gʷədəxʷšulagʷildubut ʔə tiʔił čʼχ̣ʼaʔ *Rock will not be able to get himself into the cramped space.* 3.44.

xʷiʔ [kʷi] gʷəshədʔiwʼdubuts *He won't [be able to] get himself inside.* 3.48.

xʷiʔ kʷi gʷəsbəkʷʼdxʷs *He couldn't manage [to eat] it all.* 4.23. xʷiʔəxʷ *[that there was] nothing [left] now.* 4.32

xʷi·ʔ *Nothing!* 4.80.

xʷiʔəxʷ [kʷi] gʷəsx̣ʷəs *There was no grease/fat.* 4.76.

xʷiʔəd	refuse someone/something.
xʷiʔtxʷ	cause not to be, not allow, not permit.
xʷiʔil	used up, all gone; (euphemism for) die.
xʷitʼil	fall off.
xʷitʼild	drop something, knock something off.
xʷitʼildxʷ	inadvertently drop something.
xʷitʼagʷil	rappel, lower one's self be means of block and tackle.
xʷtʼad	take something down from up high (such as decorations attached to the ceiling or a sign above the door of a store).
xʷtʼagʷil	climb down.
xʷtʼagʷiltxʷ	take/bring someone (or something) down.
xʷtʼagʷis	climb down after something/someone.
xʷtʼ-	See under xʷitʼil.

- x̣ -

x̣aʔx̣aʔ	1. that which is sacred and/or taboo 2. that which is great, mighty.
sx̣aʔx̣aʔ	in-law. tsi sx̣aʔx̣aʔ mother-in-law. sx̣a(ʔ)x̣aʔx̣aʔ in-laws.
x̣ax̣aʔx̣aʔtxʷ	forbid someone.
x̣ax̣aʔx̣aʔəd	forbid someone, caution someone.
x̣aƛʼ	want, like.
dsx̣aƛʼ	I want, I like.
x̣aƛʼtxʷ	want.
x̣aƛʼildxʷ	like someone, become fond of someone.

x̌aƛ̕il	1. argue, fight verbally 2. talk 'rough'.
x̌ayəb	laugh.
x̌ayəbdx̌ʷ	make someone laugh.
x̌ayəbid	laugh at someone.
x̌ayəbtx̌ʷ	smile at someone.
dx̌ʷx̌ayəbus	(someone) smiles.
x̌əc	afraid, scared. (x̌əc + ax̌ʷ > x̌əd²ax̌ʷ).
x̌əcdx̌ʷ	scare someone.
x̌əcbid	afraid of something/someone.
-x̌əcqg̕ʷas	pulled/cut in two (by the cinched up belt 2.59).
x̌əč	mind, feelings, understanding [The x̌əč is located in one's chest, not the head.]
x̌əčəd	count something.
x̌əčbid	think about something.
x̌əd²-	See under x̌əc.
x̌əɬ	sick. sɬəx̌ sickness. sɬiʔx̌ɬ mild sickness.
x̌əɬdx̌ʷ	hurt someone.
x̌ɬadad	a member of the family is sick.
ʔəsx̌ɬadis	sickly.
x̌əx̌ɬawil	pretend to become sick.
ʔəsx̌əɬx̌ɬil	several grow sick.
x̌əɬəɬx̌əč	broken hearted.
x̌əɬg̕ʷasbid	sick of someone, sick about something.
x̌əƛ̕	bite.
x̌əƛ̕əd	bite something/someone.
x̌ƛ̕alikʷ	bite (into something to eat). dx̌ʷsx̌ƛ̕alikʷ a biter (said of a dog).
x̌əƛ̕g̕ʷas	come together, x̌əƛ̕g̕ʷasuladx̌ʷ spring season (when the ends of the year <u>come</u> <u>together</u>).
x̌ix̌əƛ̕dup	snack, lunch.
x̌ix̌ƛ̕ustag̕ʷəl̕	converse (lit. 'nibble each other's faces').
sx̌əy̕us	head (See -ač, -qid, -us.)
x̌ib	grab, claw.

x̌ibid	grab/claw something/someone.
x̌ibx̌ib	hawk, any bird of prey.
x̌icil	angry.
x̌icis	do something to someone because of anger.
x̌icilbid	be angry with someone.
x̌iciləb	be grumpy.
x̌ikʼʷ	[See 10.8.]
x̌ƛ̓-	See under x̌əƛ̓.

- x̌ʷ -

x̌ʷalitut	snore.
x̌ʷalʼ	lack control, ʔəsx̌ʷalʼ čəd I cannot manage (something), I cannot understand (something)/figure (something) out, ʔux̌ʷalʼ čəd I was defeated, I did not get (anything) when hunting/fishing.
x̌ʷalʼbid	unable to mangage/control something or someone [x̌ʷalʼbid is the patient oriented equivalent of x̌ʷalʼ which is oriented toward the experiencer.]
x̌ʷalʼdxʷ	get the better of someone, overcome someone.
dxʷx̌ʷalʼigʷəd	give up 4.24, 4.38.
x̌ʷəlč	sea, ocean, saltchuck, Puget Sound.
(s)x̌ʷəs	fat, grease.
x̌ʷsil	grow fat, become fat.
x̌ʷsild	fatten someone, fatten up an animal.
x̌ʷulʼ	only, merely, just (this/that and nothing else), simply [predicate adverb 17.2].

- y -

syaʔyaʔ	relative, friend. syəyaʔyaʔ relatives. cəxʷsyəyaʔyaʔ in-laws.
yawʼ	only if, not until [17.2a], cəxʷyawʼ that I should 3.21.

yəhaw'txʷ — exhortation or exclamation meaning *to begin*, *to start*.

yayus — work.

yayusbid — work on something.

yəc- — tell, report, inform.

yəcəd — tell it, tell on someone, report it. **yəccut** tell about one's own experience.

yəcyid — report (something) for/in place of someone else.

yəcəb — give news. **syəcəb** news, a story, a report. **yəcəbaxʷ ʔə tiʔił bibščəb ʔi tiʔił susuqʷʼaʔs, tətyika, ʔə tiʔił słaliltubsəxʷ** (He) reported the news about Little Mink and his little younger brother, Tutyeekah, about their being brought ashore.

yəcəbid — make up a story about someone, tell about someone and embroider the details.

yəcəbyid — inform (someone) for/in place of someone else.

yəcəbtxʷ — inform someone, tell someone. **łuyəcəbtubicidəxʷ čəd** Now I will tell you (as it has been told from generation to generation).

yəhub

syəhub — traditional story, myth, **syəyəhub** [variant of **syəhub** having the same meaning].

yəhubtxʷ — recite a traditional story, **yəyəhubtxʷ** [variant of **yəhubtxʷ** having the same meaning].

yəl — both, pair.

yəlačiʔbid — use both hands on something.

yəlab — uncle or aunt of either parent when that parent is deceased. (Later, when the **yəlab** also dies, then the terms **qəsiʔ** and **ʔəpus** are used again instead of **yəlab**.)

yəl'yəlab — ancestors, parents.

yəx̌i — because.

yiq'(i)- — work into a tight place, 'worry' something into place.

yiq'id — make a cedar-root basket (patient oriented stem).

yiq'ib — make a cedar-root basket (agent oriented stem). **syiq'ib** basket (cover term).

yiq'ibad   awl for weaving cedar-root baskets.

yubil   1. starve (when the associated direct complement [16.3] represents a human being). 2. die (when the associated direct complement represents an animal).

APPENDIX

The Lushootseed sound system

There are thirty-seven consonants in the Lushootseed sound system (plus /m/ and /n/ which substitute for /b/ and /d/ in several speech styles). They utilize six positions and six manners of articulation.

	labial	alveolar	alveo-palatal			velar		uvular		glottal
stops										
plain	p	t	c	-	č	k	kʷ	q	qʷ	
glottalized	p'	t'	c'	ƛ'	č'	k'	k'ʷ	q'	q'ʷ	ʔ
voiced	b	d	dᶻ	-	ǰ	g	gʷ	-	-	
			affricates							
fricatives		s	ł	š	-	xʷ		x̌	x̌ʷ	h
				labialized						
resonants										
plain			l	y		w				
laryngealized			l'	y'		w'				
			laterals							

This consonant system is much like those in other Coast Salish languages except for the absence of nasals and the presence of a nearly complete series of voiced obstruents which are rare in Salish. The /b/ and /d/ developed from original /m/ and /n/ while both /dᶻ/ and /ǰ/ came from proto /y/. Similarly, both /g/ and /gʷ/ evolved from proto /w/. Nasals are lacking in no other Salish language except for the neighbouring Twana. The absence of /ƛ/ as a plain counterpart to /ƛ'/ is typically Salish;[57] and among the Central Coast

---

[57]Only Comox Salish has a distinct /ƛ/ which apparently entered Comox as a borrowing from a neighbouring Wakashan language.

Salish languages the lack of /x/ is also common. (In most of these languages proto /x/ shifted to /š/.)

In Lushootseed there are four vowels three of which are distinctively long and short.

high	i	u		ii	uu
		ə			
low	a			aa	

This short vowel system happens to be identical to that proposed by Laurence C. Thompson for Proto Salish.[58] Vowel length (orthographically represented by geminate letters) carries a low functional load, i.e., there are few pairs of words which are distinguished solely on the basis of long versus short vowels.

Although /ə/ is the most frequently heard sound in the language, its status is problematic. In many instances it is simply a weakly stressed variant of /a/. In other cases it is clearly epenthetic. Different from other vowels it is never long.

However, in scores of roots, the only vowel is /ə/ which, depending on suffixes present, takes major stress. Therefore, it is treated in this reader as a vowel equal to the other three whether or not it is etymologically significant.

Word stress (or 'accent') is almost but not quite completely predictable; and the system of writing Lushootseed that has come to be standard ignores stress all together. A few simple statements, however, apply to the vast majority of Lushootseed words.

Except for reduplications (discussed in the second volume) prefixes are never stressed in either Northern or Southern Lushootseed. In the north, the first vowel of a word (following prefixes) is the one receiving major stress unless that vowel is ə. If it is ə, then the first non-ə in the word is the one stressed. However, if all vowels (excluding any prefixes) are ə, then it is the first ə following prefixes that bears primary stress.

(Southern Lushootseed follows a different pattern. This series of readers, however, concerns only Northern Lushootseed, particularly as spoken at Tulalip. Therefore, the more complex rules of the south are passed over here.)

---

[58]Thompson, Laurence C. 1979. Salishan and the Northwest. Pp. 692 - 765 in *The Languages of Native North America: Historical and Comparative Assessment*. Lyle Campbell and Marianne Mithun, eds. Austin: University of Texas Press. See especially the vowels given in the chart on page 725.